TRAVELLING FREE

Also By Mandy Evans

EMOTIONAL OPTIONS
How to Use the Option Method

CHOOSING HAPPINESS
Mandy Evans Live at Interface
(Audio Cassette)

TRAVELLING FREE

How to Recover from the Past
by Changing Your Beliefs

By Mandy Evans

YES YOU CAN PRESS • 1106 Second Street #331 • Encinitas, CA 92024

Published by:
YES YOU CAN PRESS
1106 Second Street, Suite 331
Encinitas, California 92024 U.S.A.
(619) 944-6028

First Printing 1990
Printed in the United States of America

Cover by John Odam Design Associates

ISBN 1-878639-04-8 $9.95 Softcover

Library of Congress Catalog Card Number: 90-91423

There is comfort in the strength of
     love
'Twill make a thing endurable, that else
Would overset the brain, or break the heart.

William Wordsworth

To my mother, Mary,

You gave me life

and

To my son, Barnaby,

You gave me reason to live

TABLE OF CONTENTS

Learning Experiences

IMPORTANT! Read this first.

✟

Step One

How to Use This Book

This book has an unusual feature. The important part of it will come from you. It is a "how to" book in the truest sense. It will teach you how to explore issues from your past in a way that will gain you great insight into the wondrous being that you are.

The material falls into three categories:

General information — Drawn from twenty years of experience and the insight of thousands of people. See how this information matches your own insight. Use what you like of it.

Learning Experiences — Experience *is* the best teacher. Action *does* speak louder than words. When you take action and live through new experiences, you breathe life into new ideas and make them real. The "lessons" that will be most useful to you as a result of reading this book you will teach yourself by doing these exercises. People in workshops across the country have tested the exercises in this book. Some books get proof read. This one also got proof lived! The more you live it, in addition to reading it, the more you will get from it.

In choosing whether to make this the kind of book you write in or not, privacy and the intimate nature of the work you will be doing were big factors to consider. A separate notebook answered several needs. As well as the desire for privacy, it will allow you to share this book with as many people as you like.

Examples — The actual stories of the courageous people who used these ideas to free themselves from crippling and painful beliefs have been included to help you see how to use the material. Names and other details have been altered to protect their privacy.

The system for exploring beliefs used in this book is called The Option Method. It was developed by Bruce Di Marsico and popularized in several books by Barry and Suzi Kaufman. Option offers a simple, step by step method to identify beliefs that cause any form of emotional conflict, and to then explore and resolve those beliefs. Another book, **EMOTIONAL OPTIONS,** is a handbook for anyone who would like to learn how to use the Option Method for self exploration or to work with others. (See order form in the back of this book.)

When you were in school did you ever ask someone about a particular teacher, "What's this one like? Does she grade hard? Do you have to participate? Does she give pop quizzes?" Here is the best information I can provide along that line. You are the teacher.

Suggestions for Working with Yourself

1. Take good care of yourself.

2. Remember that you are the expert on your own life.

3. If you experience strong emotions, notice if they are familiar.

4. Follow instructions unless you want to do something else more.

5. Welcome confusion — It's that wonderful part of learning when you realize that things aren't the way you thought they were. It comes just before new clarity.

6. Let this be something we live together, rather than something for later or to remember. That way it will be part of us and we won't have to memorize anything.

Step Two

How This Book Came Into Being

Every four or five years, after a harsh New York winter or the bumpy ending of a love affair, California would turn into the Promised Land once again. I'd travel west looking for a home. Once again I'd return to New York, first to Manhattan, then to a small town ninety miles north of Manhattan, called Rosendale.

In that little village with the creek running through I lived in a hundred and thirty year old house on Main Street. It even had a picket fence.

I taught the Option Method for exploring and resolving the beliefs that cause emotional conflict or limit people in some way. I had taught Option for about fifteen years, to individuals and groups; it provided a foundation for the workshops I developed.

When my son, Barnaby, went off to school, the time for serious scouting for a new place to live arrived. Seven thousand miles and seven weeks of driving led to a decision at last. It took a year to sell the house, wind up my work with individual students and complete East Coast workshop commitments.

I moved to San Diego County in the Fall of 1986 and rented an apartment in Encinitas on a bluff at the edge of the world. Sunsets blazed in my windows. The Pacific Ocean roared below. In the morning, I opened my eyes to the sight of dolphins playing in the surf line.

As I walked the streets of my new home wondering how to begin again, I noticed a self-consciousness, an embarrassment at being alone. Memories flickered and strobed into awareness. There's an acting exercise called "Emotion Memory" or "Emotional Recall" in which a whole scene from the past will come forth if you catch a corner of the emotion of it, as if some inner filing system of past events sorts and stores them via emotions. I began to feel as if I'd gotten stuck in an Emotional Recall exercise. My feelings of embarrassment about being alone intensified until I actually felt ashamed to go into the same place again alone, as if everyone could tell that I was alone because I wasn't worth befriending, or, indeed, having companionship of any kind.

Somehow, I knew that it had to do with my childhood and that Adult Children of Alcoholics was the place for me to go. I remember the bitter-sweet relief of being in a room full of people who were crazy in the same particular way that I was crazy. I'd been in lots of groups, but never had I felt so strongly, "Yep, this is the one I belong to."

I listened to person after person speak openly, truthfully, simply, about his experiences in childhood—often choking with emotion and fear, but getting it out, ending the isolation and with it, the secrecy and shame for having been treated in those ways.

The flickering memories surged into vivid recollec-tions of events. I saw conclusions I had reached about those events and what they meant. A new dimension of my belief system came into view and I could perceive a structure that had molded the form my life was to take in many ways.

I cried all the way home after that first meeting. Rocking myself to sleep that night, I grieved for the frightened little girl I had been and for the opportunities to grow into a young woman with a healthy sense of self that I had lost forever because of the beliefs I had formed about myself and about my lot in life so long ago. There was a difference in the grieving this time, though. For the first time, I comforted myself . . . with a deep sense of love and affection. And I knew that I was not alone.

After several months of regular ACA meetings, I noticed that a lot of my beliefs were changing and that I was too. I had, all along, been using the Option Method to explore the beliefs I uncovered at each meeting I attended, gaining strength from the sharing of courage and love I found there.

How could I combine the possibilities for freedom and recovery I found in Option and the ACA program? The desire to make those tools available to other people like me grew and grew. First I wrote a personal article for the local San Diego ACA Sharing Letter. Then I designed a workshop which formed the basis for this book.

Knowledge grows with experience. One experience which added a lot to my understanding about travelling beyond the past occurred at a workshop in San Diego at a recovery house for alcoholics. As we explored beliefs together, a young man talked about his difficulty in eating meals with other people. First one person, then another interrupted him to commiserate or to reassure him that he'd soon be over that, or that it was just shyness; it was all to be expected, nothing to worry about. They had just about choked him off with their well meaning advice when his voice rose above theirs to say, "No, you don't understand. I have trouble eating when there are other people around because I can't keep my food on my fork. I've been eating with my hands, mostly out of cans, for the last five years. I ate my first sober meal three weeks ago." At that moment I knew that adult children of alcoholics were not the only ones with pasts to move beyond; stuff happened to all of us.

In the last three years I've learned an enormous amount from the courage, wisdom, humor and insight of the people with whom it has been my privilege to explore possibilities for healing. They've confirmed that it is possible for every one of us to greet each new day more freely. With an expanding ability to accept ourselves and to trust ourselves just the way we are, life becomes a very different journey, one that we can enjoy *now* (even before we fix everything we believe needs changing).

Here is some of what we discovered together.

Step Three

The Power of Acceptance

There is only one starting place that I know of. It's here and now: two of the least popular locations in time and space.

For example, a young woman I worked with in New York had a rough time supporting herself while she studied for a career as an opera singer. She expressed angry impatience about the obstacles she encountered. She was especially angry about waiting on tables in order to pay her bills and furious about her predicament in general. The idea of accepting her situation fueled the fires of fury.

"Maybe you can't get there from here." I said, referring to the journey from angry waitress to "debuting-diva." Her response came promptly and loudly. "Well, where the hell can I get there from?"

Asking, "Where can I go from here? What step can I take now?" (since it's only from *here* that I can take any steps at all) would probably take us further down the road.

In moving beyond the past, it helps to see where we are now and to accept that. Please note, the word is *accept*, not *resign* yourself to less than you want. To accept means to receive with consent. There's nothing about a contract or promise to keep anything forever. You can still reach for anything you want, change anything you like. When you accept this moment, you free yourself to move in any direction you choose. You avoid using your energy to fight with what has already happened. What-has-already-happened doesn't care what we think about it. It just is.

Let us respect our relationship to the past as we experience it now. We carry memories and beliefs with us. Those memories and beliefs can guide us. They can heal us and nurture us, or they can torture us and, we are beginning to learn, they can kill us. We often view new events through the same system that took us in that direction in the first place. What occurs then validates our conclusions from the past because that's how we see things.

24

What We See Is Mostly
What We Look For

Rebecca spent most of her adult life looking for rejection. She sat in a circle on a folding chair in a converted barn at one of the Beyond the Past workshops. Her very pale skin contrasted dramatically with her very black hair. Rebecca trailed an impressive list of accomplishments behind her. She referred to them frequently.

"I just can't take the rejection any more," she said tearfully. "It just hurts too much." I asked her what she meant by rejection. She looked bewildered. I explained that the question was not meant as a challenge but to help us understand more about her experience, that each of us was unique and that rejection meant different things to different people.

"Well," she replied, "like if I call somebody and they don't call me back. Or I invite someone to do something two or three times and they don't invite me to do something, if I always have to call them. Or if I pay someone a nice compliment, I always try to think of something nice to say to people, and they don't say anything nice about me."

I was genuinely puzzled. "Why do you see those things as rejection?" I asked. The Option Dialogue that followed went like this:

25

A. "Because it might be a rejection."

Q. "If it might be a rejection, why do you look for it?"

A. "To protect myself from it." Tears came again. "I really don't think I can take much more of it. I've been rejected all my life."

Q. "How does looking for rejection protect you from it?"

A. After a very long pause Rebecca said in a drifting away voice, "It helps me to avoid it."

Q. "Do you believe that?"

A. "Do I believe what?" As Rebecca confronted the belief she had held for so long, that looking for rejection would help her to avoid rejection, it was hard for her to even hear the question, much less answer it.

Q. "Do you believe that looking for rejection helps you to avoid rejection?"

A. "That sounds kind of crazy, doesn't it?" She chuckled. "Maybe that's why I feel so rejected all the time. I see it everywhere."

An answering chuckle and a sigh of relief came from the group. From that point, Rebecca could explore a whole host of beliefs about rejection. Our acceptance of her coupled with gently probing questions to find out more about what she believed allowed her to see herself and her actions in a softer, brighter light.

Here's the predicament. You're probably reading this because you want to change some stuff. The idea of acceptance is fine, but what about all of those things that you really do want to change? Why would you want to accept what you're trying to change? We wage an internal war with the parts of our lives we want to correct. We take a firm position (against those feelings, or memories or aspects of our personalities) and hold it tight, as if we were arm wrestling with it. That kind of striving makes it seem dangerous to relax for a moment and risk losing the leverage or momentum we might never recapture. That might be a good way to arm wrestle; it can prove a debilitating approach to life. Can you imagine what would happen if you required the muscles of your right arm to engage in permanent combat with the muscles of your left arm?

Acceptance allows change. The acceptance mode includes everything, even my judgments. It allows me to be okay now, even before I reach my goals. Acceptance permits happiness, clear perception and love. An attitude of acceptance offers a starting point for healing, learning, finding new directions. It provides a foundation from which to reach and grow.

When you begin to accept yourself the way you are right now, you begin a new life with new possibilities that did not exist before because you were so caught in the struggle against reality that that was all you could do.

There may not be a greater gift you can bestow on yourself or a friend than to listen, quietly and openly. It allows profound healing to take place. Into that quiet receptivity pours a stream of words, memories, thoughts, feelings. A kind of communion results that differs from the everyday musings and wheel-spinnings that fill our minds and wear us out.

Learning Experience One

Listening With Acceptance

Find a quiet, comfortable place to be and get a pen or pencil. You may want to get a special notebook to use for these exercises. It can be your *Travelling Free Journal*.

Ask yourself: "What has been hard for you in the past?"

Give yourself at least 10 minutes with that question. Let the memories float up at their own rate. Write down what you want to. Just hang out with the question and listen to yourself. You don't have to fix anything, or even understand it . . . just allow the inquiry to move through you. Whatever your response is, treat yourself respectfully. Tears, laughter, words, thoughts, images, are all fine responses. All you have to do is ask yourself "What has been hard for you in the past?" and receive the response, the gift of self-revelation.

This is an exercise you can do many times. It will reward you with the gift of self-knowledge. It will help you to allow things to creep out of the shadows. It is important to regard yourself and the material that comes forth gently and with affection — the way you would watch a baby learning to walk — doing his very best, but stumbling, falling, leaning over too far, going too fast and falling down. Would you judge him harshly for the way he learns? Or is his innocent striving endearing and delightful to behold?

Take time to look over what you've written. Reading it is different from writing it. Seeing your words provides a new perspective and allows you to access the information in different ways. Remind yourself to let this be a time-out from having to understand and fix yourself. Just be here. See what you see. Remember what you remember. Feel what you feel.

If you want to travel free, if you'd like to drop all excess baggage, make accepting yourself and others the first step. Acceptance is not resignation; acceptance is love.

＋

Step Four

What Happened to You?

(And why was it hard for you?)

Sometimes, in the attempt to free themselves from pain, people try to forget the past, or gloss it over. Or they tell themselves that they "should be over that by now" or that "it wasn't really so bad." Denial never works. It doesn't change anything; it *prevents* anything from changing.

There's a saying, "It can't hurt more to know and not remember than it does to remember." In Learning Experience One, you may have remembered things you had forgotten or remembered them differently.

We're going to learn how to discover liberating truths in those memories, so that you can change the way that they affect you now if you want to. We're going to focus on a particular example from your life so that you can learn more about the underlying causes of the emotional pain and self-imposed limits you live with.

Learning Experience Two

Exploring the Hard Part

Choose one thing that has been hard for you in your life.

Make sure it could end in: "_____ _____ was hard for me."
Or "_____, that was hard for me."

Writing your responses in that way will help you to work with them. Sometimes you'll get a phrase, sometimes a paragraph. Keep it simple.

Here are some examples people have used in workshops:

• <u>Being overweight</u> was hard for me.

• <u>When I was a kid, I'd try to help my father when he worked on stuff. And you know, you loved him so much. Sometimes he'd haul off and hit me so hard I'd pee in my pants.</u> That was hard for me.

- <u>When my father left for war and never came back</u> was hard for me.

- <u>My daughter was raped and there was nothing I could do to change it or help her.</u> That was hard for me.

- <u>Always trying to be good enough so that I'd be safe</u> was hard for me.

Write down one thing that was hard for you.

Ask: "What was hard for you about that?" Dare to question the obvious. The answers may not be so obvious. People sometimes look at me, aghast when I ask, "What was hard for you about that?" referring to the suicide of a mother or the loss of a job. On occasion an agitated person blurts out, "How can you ask such a dumb question?!" Ask because even though such an event might be difficult for anyone, it *means* something different to different people. The question is not intended to challenge you or your beliefs. It is meant to shed light in the corners where you never look.

Do at least 5 examples in order to see the relationship between what happened and what was hard for you about it more clearly.

Now you know more about what made
your example difficult or painful for you.

Next we'll begin to explore the sense you
made from the seeming evidence at hand.
Here's where your past truly can change!
The conclusions you came to when you
were three years old and have lived by ever
since, might not seem valid at all if you look
at them now. That can hold true for a conclusion that you came to five minutes ago
as well.

ﾔ

Step Five

What Did It Mean?

The meaning we attribute to the events and circumstances in our lives gives form to our perception of those events. That meaning determines how we react emotionally. If you think something endangers you, you will react differently from the way you will if you believe that a blessing awaits. This ascribed meaning often goes un-noticed as the intensity of our pain summons our attention and we search for ways to escape the feelings. The conclusions we come to about ourselves, our lives, our chances for happiness hurt more than any event in and of itself. It is the beliefs that keep the pain alive long after the situation has gone.

A Betrayal of Trust — What Did It Mean?

For instance, two attractive young women, Beth and Amy had each at different times, become romantically involved with their high school English teacher. He introduced them to romantic literature, poetry—the exquisite intimacy a writer creates with his reader. This man pursued a romantic, and to some extent sexual, relationship with each girl and then ended it abruptly in order to focus his attention on another student who then became his favorite. Each teenage girl suffered pain. Each felt humiliated. For each, it involved a loss of self esteem, of spontaneity, of youthful exuberance. Both women even used the exact same words to describe the event . . . "and then he dumped me."

But it only seems as if the same thing happened to both of them. It meant something different to each of them. That meaning caused their pain. That meaning became their doorway to freedom.

BETH sat opposite me on a comfortable couch. When I asked at one point, "What was hard for you about that?" she gazed out of the window at the palm fronds drooping over the fence and the magenta bougainvillea in the back yard.

Long straight blond hair framed her face. She pulled it out from behind; it draped across one shoulder as she leaned forward. She rested her arms on her long legs and looked at the floor. Beth had come to see me because she wanted to drop out of college and feared making a bad choice. Our talks led to painful memories of her days in high school. "I felt like such a fool!" Anger rang in her voice. "I felt like I couldn't trust anybody ever again. I thought I couldn't trust myself either. That was the worst part. I didn't even have me! I thought I couldn't tell what to do. I couldn't tell what was good for me and," with a wry grimace, "what wasn't! So now," she said bitterly, "I just go to school and study hard and get A's and get more student loans and get deeper in debt. I feel like I've been doing it forever and I'm so sick of it."

Some of the core conclusions or beliefs that Beth identified were:

- "I can't trust myself to tell what's good for me."
- "If I quit school, I'll be lost."
- "If I weren't hurt and angry, it would mean I didn't care what happens to me."

As Beth explored those beliefs they crumbled away. During the next few weeks, she uncovered and unravelled still more beliefs from the past. She decided that she could trust her strong desire to leave school at the end of that semester. She added some travel and some adventure to her life. She hiked in mountains, studied for the pure joy of learning and took workshops to expand her knowledge of herself. Several years later she returned and completed her master's degree. Beth now works as a guidance counselor in a high school.

AMY came to see me because she wanted to return to school and was afraid. She knew she was smart but, in her words, she had "crashed and burned" under the pressure of going to a local junior college. The experience of a new environment, all new people, and new schedules overwhelmed her. She sank into a fear-filled depression and missed one class, then another. Soon the idea of confronting all of those missed classes loomed too big to deal with. She stopped going altogether. She felt isolated and ashamed. The under-achiever label stuck to Amy the same way over-achiever was used to characterize Beth. Amy's appearance also contrasted sharply with Beth's. She was short and a little plump while Beth looked like a young colt. Amy wore her dark hair short, in tousled curls.

Amy's conversation also led to a high school experience which she had never told anyone about before.

"We used to read poetry together and go for long walks in the woods. Sometimes he'd kiss me. I thought I was special." Amy still smiled softly as she remembered that happy time in her life. "Then he dumped me." The cold sound of finality silenced other noises. The room filled with silence.

I waited. When the intensity of the moment softened, I asked, "What was hard for you about that?"

"I felt so ashamed." she said, simply.

"What did you feel ashamed about?" I asked.

"That he dumped me," she whispered.

"What did that mean to you?" I probed gently, as if stroking a bruise to see how tender it is.

"It meant that I was nothing. That I was less than nothing. That no one would ever want me because I was just nothing."

Amy's hands covered her face. Her tears fell between her fingers. The words had come out in little bursts, three or four at a time, with long quiet stretches in between. Sneakered feet rubbed rhythmically back and forth on the carpet. Her voice trembled with anger and pain and shame. She seemed very young, about fourteen.

41

"Do you believe that?" I asked after a few moments. Amy's body relaxed slowly. She leaned back against the couch. A soft smile moved her face and my heart.

"No, I don't," she said, the same softness in her voice, "He just wanted to live a love poem. I can understand that. I wanted to live a love poem too."

Amy returned to school. Several years later when she learned that her former teacher had applied for a job that would put him in close contact with women who were in crisis, she came forward and spoke up against his being hired. She spoke without bitterness or rancor. She stood her ground against his strong counter attack and stated simply that she wished him no harm. She just didn't think it was a good idea for him to be in that position with women who might be vulnerable and told the hiring committee why.

Sweet freedom! Both Amy and Beth moved forward free from the belief, "I'm nothing, less than nothing" and the belief, "I can't trust my own judgement." Amy returned to school; Beth left. Both felt genuinely good about themselves.

These young women moved forward to create far different lives from the ones they fashioned while believing that they couldn't count on themselves or were not worthy of love and caring, both in terms of inner experiences and outer circumstances.

Learning Experience Three

The Pain Is In The Meaning

Take the example from your life that you've been exploring. If you use the same one, you can trace the chain that links experience-perception-belief to a way-of-life more clearly. You will be able to see how those elements work together to create your very life. There was something that was hard for you. You know more about what was hard *about* that experience now. And more about how to accept yourself and your life as you rummage about in it.

Use your sentence from the last Learning Experience. It began:

" _____ was hard for me."
Or " _____, that was hard for me."

Ask: What did it mean to you then?

Ask: What does it mean to you now?

Again, take as much time as you like to be with this question. Let the question roam around in your consciousness, your memories, your body. Notice what you find. Write down the part that will fit into words so that you can see them.

Υ

Step Six

Heavy Baggage

Now that you can take something that was hard for you in your life and find out *what* was hard about it and what it meant to you, the next step is to find out how an experience from your past and the conclusions you came to about it might affect you now.

For example, a boy we'll call Tom and his brother, Jeff, grew up in a chaotic, violent family. Both kids retreated into their own worlds. Communication broke down between them. Each boy faced his fear and shame about the family alone, convinced that he had no one to turn to. Both brothers learned to guard the secrets of their homelife from other people.

In adulthood both Tom and Jeff have extreme difficulty with close relationships. The older brother, Tom, found a career in the Marines where he could belong without having to communicate about his private life. Tom likes to know as much as possible about what will happen. He finds his key to feeling safe in predictable outcomes. He welcomes the orderly environment and discipline of military life. Another person might see him as rigid and uncommunicative; he might be described as up-tight.

The younger brother, Jeff, struggles with a cocaine habit and a series of disastrous relationships with women. He resents any kind of authority as if he upholds a vow that he will never again place himself at the mercy of someone else's power. That decision and the belief in its importance for his well-being shape Jeff's life as surely as a mold shapes plaster.

The experiences of being beaten and humiliated as children influence each brother differently today. Becoming aware of how events from your past affect you today will mark a path you can follow that leads to freedom. It will wind through feelings and beliefs and bring you to the present with less baggage than you had when you began the journey. You won't have to part with anything you need for the trip.

There Is No Greater Burden Than a Tool That Is No Longer Useful

We often view new events through the same system that took us in that direction in the first place. The new events then validate our conclusions from the past because that's how we see things.

Here is an example of a man who used fear as a tool to help himself avoid failure. At a workshop in New York, I once asked a group of people if there was anything they wouldn't want to feel okay about.

The title of the workshop was "Choice and Motivation." A man raised his hand. He explained that he had lost a lot of money in the stock market. When I asked him, "How do you feel about that?" he replied, "Awful. I feel really awful, like I'm a failure. I feel guilty and I'm afraid I'll make a big mistake again. It haunts me. It's with me all the time." The following dialogue went like this:

> **Q.** Imagine that I have a magic wand. If I wave it, your fear will disappear, and you will feel okay about what happened, do you want me to wave it?

47

A. No!

Q. Why not?

A. Because I might do it again.

Q. Do what again?

A. What I did before. (He was getting irritated with me at this point.)

Q. What did you do before?

A. (In exasperation, he huffed out . . .) I'd be careless. I'd repeat what I did and I'd lose a lot of money . . . and I don't have a lot of money to lose right now!

Q. Do you believe that?

A. Yes! (He was genuinely disgusted with me by then.)

Q. You would? Knowing what you know now? If you weren't afraid, you'd make the same investment all over again?

A. Well, not the same investment. I know about that. But I might do it with one I didn't know about.

Q. How would being afraid help you deal with an investment you don't know about?

People began to chuckle. He didn't even hear them. He mused, lost in thought. Slowly a bewildered smile appeared, replacing the irritated expression.

> **A.** It wouldn't help me. In fact, it hurts me. When I'm afraid, it's hard for me to learn. It's hard to concentrate. I can't pay attention. I can't be alert. I'd never make a mistake on purpose. (He beamed with delight now.) Being scared all the time wouldn't help me to avoid mistakes at all! Do you really have a magic wand? (He laughed right out loud.)

That man gave us such a clear example of how a conclusion about an event can influence the rest of your life. He believed he had to be afraid in order to prevent another disastrous mistake. He lived with that possibility. It surrounded him, waiting to get him at any moment. The very thing that he did to protect himself increased the likelihood of his making an error in financial judgement because his fear made it impossible to assess possibilities accurately.

His face looked so different. He looked younger, more confident, relaxed, alive. And I hadn't even waved the wand.

Learning Experience Four

How Does Your Past Affect You Now?

Choose something to focus on.

It can be anything you want to know more about. It's like learning how to hammer a nail. It doesn't matter what nail you choose to use first; once you know how to do it you can hammer any nail you like.

Write down one thing that was hard for you in the past.

Ask yourself: How does that affect you now?

Take as long as you want with this question. It helps to stay with it a bit longer when you think you're ready to move on. That allows more to come forward — more insight, more consciousness. If, for instance, it was hard for you when a love relationship ended, how does that affect you now? Or, if you suffered a business loss, how does that affect you now?

If you experience strong emotions while doing this, notice if they are familiar. The goal here, is to locate the pain, (or anger, or guilt, or shame) not to cause it!

Let the feelings wash through you.

There's nothing you have to do about them right now. Remember that tears heal the pain. They are not the pain itself. Biologists have found that the chemical make-up of tears of emotion differs from the content of the tears of eye irritation. Tears of grief, for example contain a substance that functions much like morphine. How ironic that we come equipped with physical attributes to help us deal with life and that we then (in our confusion) suppress the very functions meant to help us.

Look through what you've written so far. See if you can spot the beliefs you have expressed. Read like a detective hunting for clues that point to conclusions you came to.

Underline or highlight statements you recognize as beliefs. Remember a belief is simply a perception of reality, a conclusion you came to, or something you were told and had no reason not to accept. Becoming aware of what you believe is one of the most potentially liberating experiences a person can have. Often, when people discover that something they have believed is simply not true for them, they dissolve feelings of anger, guilt, fear and self-doubt that have seemed inevitable — sometimes for years.

$\curlyvee$

Step Seven

What Do You Believe?

It's not what happens to us, so much as what we come to believe, that shapes our lives. Stuff happens to everyone and some of it is not what we would want for ourselves or anybody else. Maybe what hurts you still or limits your life now, is the conclusions you came to and the beliefs you formed from the *seeming* evidence at hand.

We can learn to identify self-defeating beliefs to see if they hold true for us now. You can begin to recognize the self-created restrictions that you've imposed since you were a small child and may not have questioned since. There is a way to determine the underlying cause of your pain and frustration so that you may remedy it.

A group of little kids were playing trolley together. They took turns reaching into the air above their heads to ring the imaginary bell and let the trolley-man know he had arrived at their stop and they wanted to get off. At one point one small passenger bolted from the trolley and ran crying to his mother. When he found her, he sobbed, "They won't let me ring the bell!"

He believed the other kids could stop him from ringing a bell that he had created with his own imagination. What are the bells you can't ring because you believe there's something stopping you that isn't it really there? What do you believe that hurts you or limits you now? What did you come to believe about what happened to you in the past?

A belief is simply:

- A perception of reality or truth
- A conclusion you come to
- Something we are told that we have no reason not to accept. So simple, but so powerful. Our beliefs tell us what to do, how to feel, what *is*. When beliefs change — and they can in a flash, whole new vistas open to us. New directions become possible that we could not perceive before.

56

Emily's Beliefs

Emily, for example, grew up in a violent, angry household. Her parents struggled bitterly to make ends meet. They told her how bad rich people were and how "they" don't care about "us." When she asked for toys or clothes in her eager little girl voice they countered with harsh accusations about how greedy she was. Emily believed, among other things, that asking for what she wanted only made things worse and that people who had extra wouldn't want to give any to her. She learned to feel shame about being poor. She concluded that she was somehow worth less than other children. She believed that wanting things hurt. She learned to give up. She learned to tolerate abuse in stoic silence. If there were a test on "How Things Really Are" Emily would have failed it hands down. She was a bright, attractive child with many talents. Her conclusions and her beliefs were real to her, though, and she lived by them.

But she never learned how to crush the desire to love and be loved out of her own throbbing heart. It goes right on beating and the yearning she feels, combined with the emotional pain her beliefs caused, made Emily want to die to escape from it. She learned to protect herself from the pain she felt when she encountered those beliefs by withdrawing into lonely isolation.

As a young woman, Emily struggles endlessly with money problems about which she feels a constant deep shame. She rarely asks anyone for anything. Instead she tries to be good enough to deserve favors, attention, love. She manipulates, whines a little. A cloudy petulance dims the brightness of her eyes and makes her smile a bit tense. Once in a great while she builds a solid case against someone for not giving her what she wants and explodes in rage. She tolerates mistreatment in all of her relationships, so she gets far more than the normal share.

Because of her beliefs, Emily lives in a harsh, uncaring, world, in which she encounters little of generosity, kindness, respect, loyalty, fun or anything that makes it worth getting up in the morning.

Most of what Emily does to help herself works against her at this point.

As her beliefs change, she learns to identify what she wants rather than to focus on avoiding pain. When Emily begins to ask for what she wants, her whole life transforms. The circumstances begin to validate new beliefs. It's not easy. It seems at times as if all reality is crumbling away and that there's nothing to hold onto. Her terror about asking for what she wants almost chokes her. It feels life-threatening to hope, to want, to express her desire.

And in a way it is. It does threaten the only life Emily has known and she doesn't know what she will be like if it changes.

Emily moves at her own pace, learning to accept herself as she goes. A major breakthrough occurred when she caught herself wanting to end her current relationship and building a case against her boyfriend for not caring about her. Instead of doing without, she asked her boyfriend to chip in on expenses for the dinners she cooks. His delight at being asked and his willingness to contribute amazed her. Her reality shifts, slightly at first, but little by little she creates a new belief system. As she lives within the structure of that belief system the things that happen to her are different from the things that happened to her when she lived by the conclusions from her past.

What do you believe:

- about yourself?
- about life?
- about your chances for happiness?
- about what you can accomplish?

What conclusions did you draw from the _seeming_ evidence at hand, that hurt you or limit you today?

You have some material to work with now. You have thoughts, feelings, memories, images from the past, ideas, conclusions, the sensations in your body—valuable information about your beliefs.

Learning Experience Five

Self-Defeating Beliefs

Your own beliefs may surprise you. Mine do. We seem to have filed them in all sorts of complicated ways. Some are top secret, others hopelessly mis-filed; there are those that pop up all the time whether we like it or not.

With affection and self-acceptance, look to see what you really do believe, rather than to find out if you believe the right thing. You can't determine what "the right thing" to believe is out of context or by trying to accept someone else's belief system. You can try to believe "the right thing," but your real belief will still be there and the two beliefs create all kinds of conflict. Find out *what* you believe before you try to change it. Remember, your belief is your perception of reality.

Ask: What do you believe that may hurt you or limit you now?

Give yourself at least ten quiet minutes to see what occurs to you.

61

Listen to yourself. There's a thread that winds through your life; you are the only one who can follow it. Only you know what your experiences mean to you. You are the one who can discover what you believe and why.

See if you can find at least 10 self-defeating beliefs.

Here is a belief that caused a good deal of unhappiness in my own life — one that shaped my life in many ways because of the choices I made in keeping with that concept of reality. Holding this belief caused a perpetual self-consciousness, a wariness and a sense of shame. No amount of reassurance from the outside softened the intensity of those feelings, though I tried that approach with varying degrees of desperation. More often, I hid my fears. I hid my anger. I concealed every desire in layers of manipulative favors granted to people I hoped would then need me enough to care for me. I buried ambition. I disguised extreme swings of mood and energy level until they burst forth in near psychotic episodes of rage and despair. This would usually occur in relationships, when I was with some poor guy whom I had nominated best candidate for "Knight with White Charger."

I'm Not Good Enough to Have a Father

That belief surfaced one night as I sat with a group of students in my living room in Rosendale N.Y. We shared beliefs that had somehow stunted our growth. "I believe I'm not good enough to have a father." I said matter-of-factly, taking my turn. A couple of people smiled or nodded understanding. The next person spoke.

"Do I believe that?" I wondered as the group continued to share their beliefs. "Yes . . .Yes?" I startled myself. "Yes I do." "I do?" I asked again, incredulously. By now I was smiling to myself. "Why do I believe that?" The belief crumbled away in absurdity. "Mass murderers have fathers," I thought. "Mothers and fathers rear all sorts of children." I never struggled to convince myself that I deserved fatherly love again. The issue simply disappeared, although I continue to find little off-shoots, little belief-lets that grew from the main root and show up from time to time when I least expect them.

In that moment I knew that I did, indeed, have a father, an alcoholic one who had loved me very much. He wasn't the greatest guy to hang around with a lot of the time, especially for a little kid. He's dead now, but he was, and is, my father, mine all mine. I still can't tell whether I'm good or not; I can't quite get the criteria down pat. I do know that being good and having a father are not related in the way I had them hooked up.

When you question your own beliefs, be patient and gentle with yourself. Make your questions genuine inquiries, not disguised statements about what a dunce you are. If someone asked you a question designed to prove what a jerk you were, you wouldn't answer freely and comfortably; perhaps you wouldn't answer at all. You won't answer yourself if you ask that way either.

If you get confused, if the very gears in your brain seem to seize, you have probably located an excellent belief to explore. There's only one technical term in this method. It's called "Getting Stupid." Somehow when we confront our own belief systems things get very foggy for awhile. We may as well have asked, "How hot is that ice?" The question makes no sense what-so-ever. If you've hit a really good belief — nothing else makes much sense at that moment either.

Most of us haven't got a storehouse of happy memories of times when we were asked a question and then felt completely confused. And yet confusion is a natural, wonderful state which occurs when we realize that things aren't the way we thought they were and just before we see the new answer.

Wouldn't it be wonderful if children were encouraged to shout out their confusion gleefully in school. "Ooohhhh, I'm so confused! I must really be learning!" instead of striving to hide it fearfully.

When I work with people, I sometimes have to ask the same question five or ten times before they can even hear it.

Question the obvious. Sometimes when I ask people a question like, "What was hard for you about that?" they look at me aghast. They say things like, "Wouldn't it be hard for anyone?" Sometimes they get very angry. Perhaps they heard the question as a challenge. Maybe they have learned to protect their inner-most thoughts with anger. That emotion deserves respect and exploration too.

It might be hard for anyone if his mother committed suicide. The break-up of a marriage may be painful for anyone. But it will be difficult for each person in a different way, for different reasons. Each person attaches different interpretations to such an event because of his own life experiences, beliefs, and what he wants for himself. Each person is unique. It's that uniqueness we wish to respect with the question, "What was hard for you about that?" The question leads to insight, not a challenge to your right to your beliefs and feelings.

Learning Experience Six

Exploring Beliefs — The Healing Dialogue

Use this Option Method exercise to explore your beliefs to see if they still hold true for you.

Choose one of your beliefs to explore. Use this form to help you to be sure that it is a belief: I believe ___(fill in the blank)___ . It doesn't matter which one. Remember it's like hammering nails. Once you know how, you can hammer lots of different kinds of nails.

Ask yourself these questions and write down the answers.

- Do I believe that?

- Why do I believe that?

- Is it true?

All answers are correct.

- Maybe

- I don't know

- Yes

- No

These are all fine answers.

Now ask yourself: What might happen if I didn't believe that? Write down your answer; it might be a long one.

Then ask: Would that be okay?

In the earlier example, we didn't get to the last question, "What might happen if I didn't believe that?" A young man asked that as he explored his belief that he wasn't good enough to be loved. He answered, "I wouldn't be careful to be good." He thought for a moment, then he cracked up. "I doubt that I'd get really out of hand after all these years of goodness-training. I might even be more lovable if I weren't so damned careful all the time." He smiled. "You know," he said, "I really do have values. And I like them! I guess that's all I need to know. I'm so tired of being afraid I'm unworthy all the time. Maybe people will just like me or not and I can stop guessing for awhile and see what happens." A very long pause followed. His voice held a chuckle when he said, "I don't think I've been *all that good* either if we're going to tell the truth here . . . just always scared of getting caught."

One by one the beliefs dissolve. The pain eases. The wounds heal.

TOP 20

ALL-TIME MOST POPULAR
SELF-DEFEATING BELIEFS SO FAR

1. I'm not good enough to be loved.

2. No matter what I do, I should be doing something else.

3. I can tell what *will* happen by what *has* happened.

4. If it hasn't happened yet, it never will.

5. If I were happy, I wouldn't do anything.

6. I upset people.

7. Asking for what you want is scary, very scary.

8. I should have worked this out by now.

9. If you know what I'm really like, you won't want me.

10. Better stop wanting; if you get your hopes up, you'll just get hurt.

11. If I fail, I should feel bad for a very long time and be really scared to try again.

12. If there's something you don't like about yourself, (it's best to) hide it and hate it.

13. Sex is dirty and nasty; save it for the one you love.

14. I can't trust myself.

15. I don't know what I want.

16. If I become unhappy now, it will save me from becoming unhappy later.

17. If I'm grown up no one will ever help me. I'll be all alone if I really need help.

18. The one I'm with now is the only one who would ever want me and I'm not sure how long I can fool him/her.

19. Everyone else knows something that's wrong with me and they won't tell me.

20. I want bad things for myself.

Learning Experience Seven

Your Own Top Twenty

Go though the twenty beliefs listed. Note the ones that you believe.

Create your own Top Twenty list. Find twenty things you believe that might prove limiting, self-defeating or cause emotional pain.

For each belief, ask yourself: Why do you believe that?

What might happen if you didn't believe that?

Do you think it's true?

✛

Step Eight

Is There Something You Could Do or Say?

Here's the good news, you *can* change the past, at least you can change the part that counts, the part you carry with you. At one workshop, a woman we'll call Sue, told us about a sorrow she felt trapped with like a life sentence. Sue discovered that her only child, a girl we'll call Karen) had been involved in a complicated sexual relationship since her early teens. The man was about twenty years older than Karen. He was also married to Sue's cousin.

When the involvement was discovered all hell broke loose. Sue and her cousin argued bitterly. The man denied everything. Karen felt terribly ashamed. She withdrew into a world of drugs and her own kind of insanity that had been diagnosed as schizophrenia at one point.

Sue suffered from the loss of her relationship with her cousin. The two women had been best friends for a long time. Since they were little girls they had shared secrets, adventures, triumphs and losses as they grew up together in a small town.

An almost all-pervading guilt weighed on Sue's being like a heavy cloak she could not take off. She suspected that neglect played a part in the whole mess. As a single parent with a career as an attorney she had spent long hours away from Karen. She questioned the values that might have placed material security above closeness and time spent together. Sue further tortured herself with recriminations about her own failed marriage. She blamed her own choice of husbands for the lack of nurturing male guidance in Karen's life. She judged herself mercilessly for the lack of communication that kept her unaware of Karen's secret affair for so long.

When I asked Sue what was hard for her about that, she answered, "That I can't do anything about it. My cousin is so angry with me. I don't know how to help my daughter. And I feel so guilty that I let it happen."

As we explored what had happened and what she believed together, a definite shift occurred. She began to talk about how close she and Karen had become, in contrast to those years when she had struggled so hard to provide material things, caught up in a whirlwind pursuit of success as a single parent. Then we delved into beliefs about what the future might hold for Karen. Sue imagined a living hell for her child to endure . . . with no end in sight. She could envision no other outcome from the events and circumstances that she described.

We questioned those beliefs also. Together, we made our way through the perceptions, and assumptions about how things work that she had been taught and never questioned for herself. We travelled through the emotional and physical pain and came to a clearing where she could begin to want more for herself and her daughter than a lifetime of suffering. One belief Sue uncovered was that she, herself had to live with guilt and regret in order to know that she cared about her child. That belief dissolved easily.

When asked simply, "Do you love Karen and care about her?" she felt the love in her heart and nodded yes without a pause. "Do you have any reason to believe that you would stop loving Karen and caring about her well-being if your guilt and regret went away?"

When one version of reality breaks up and another emerges something happens that is hard to describe but can be felt by everyone. We *felt* it when Sue realized that she could feel her love even more strongly *without* regret. When she was happy it was so easy to think of Karen and be with her. When she was miserable, Sue dreaded being with her daughter. She felt guilty about that, but the dread didn't go away. It was also easier to find creative ways to help Karen get on with her life when Sue felt good herself.

When we finished working together Sue radiated love and hope. The full, rich, happy life she so much wanted for Karen seemed as possible as any other future Sue could imagine. A glance around at the shining faces in the room confirmed that others saw that possibility as completely real too.

At that point a man of about 70 years told us what had happened to him when his son died of cancer at a young age. The man talked about the anger and fear that his son felt in his last days. He told us how much his son had wanted to live and how helpless he had felt as a father when he sat with his child.

He had gone to his synagogue to pray. The comfort and insight that he found there had started him on a different path in his life. His religious work had become an important part of his life and he had founded a center that had helped lots of people. "I feel his presence" he said, "to this day. Only it's peaceful now. Just love."

The room was hushed, with a feel, more than a sound, of gentle stirring — like a rustle. People actually looked up and around. No one spoke. The room filled with love. The light changed and the difference was visible to everyone. "I never told anyone about those feelings," the man said. "The past does change. It's not a tragedy to me that he died anymore."

If something from your past seems to stick to you like glue. If there's something you just can't shake. If, for example, there's something you tell yourself to let go of, and you let go of it, only it's still there, so you let go of it again, and it's still there . . . maybe you can't let go because there's something you can do or say that would be good for you. Would you want to give up in resignation if there were some way to complete the issue or resolve a conflict so that you could then let it rest with satisfaction? If you trusted yourself to want what's best for you, you could stop trying to let go of it and find out more about it.

Maybe there's someone you want to tell how much he has meant to you. Or maybe you have a parent that you always wanted to have listen to you just once and really hear what you have to say. Whether the person is alive or dead, there may be something you want to do or say in some area of your life that just won't rest until you do. Or maybe it's a matter you never completed with yourself.

Perhaps you can't let it rest because you want something that you don't easily allow yourself to want or something that you believe is impossible. When we judge our wanting we can try to squeeze it out of our own hearts. It hurts, but the wanting doesn't usually die that easily. There is nothing more painful that I know of, than trying to wrench the desire from your own heart. What might happen if you respected and trusted yourself enough to know that if you can't let go, you probably have a reason to hold on? Perhaps all we lack is information and clarity.

Recently a friend asked, "How do you know when to let go?" "When you want to hold something else more," I offered.

Learning Experience Eight

When to Let Go

Ask yourself: Is there something you've been trying to let go of without success?

"What is it?"

"Is there something you could do or say? If you had permission to follow your wanting, where would it guide you?"

When you have that answer, ask: "Do you want to do that or say that?"

Here are some things you can do or say in order to complete an issue from your past.

- Write a letter. The person you write to can be alive or dead. You never have to mail it, but you can if you want to later.

- Draw a mandala with magic markers, water colors, crayons, whatever. Draw a circle and fill it up. You can use a turned over plate or bowl with a light pencil to outline the circumference.

81

Focus on a particular relationship or issue from your past that clings to you as if it had a life of its own. Draw your feelings in the circle. You may use symbols, colors, rhythms, anything that visually expresses your truth. Whatever ends up in that circle is perfect for your mandala.

• If another person is involved, write down what you would like for that person to know — *not* what you want to tell that person — what you would want the person to know if the telling fairy could come and do the telling.

• Ask yourself what might happen to you if you no longer had this issue in your life? Is there any way it would be bad for you if you were free from it?

Step Nine

A Brand New Day

When you turn your focus to *this* moment the world changes. It becomes new. From this new moment the pulling and tugging of buried hopes and desires begin to lose some of their strength as you explore and resolve them.

What might your life be like if you trusted yourself to want only good things? What if you trusted your desire, your wanting, your awareness of what would be welcome to you, as if it were an inner sense of direction that would guide you through life perfectly, providing you with every experience needed along the way for your perfect development and happiness?

Perhaps everything we truly want is readily available to us and all we need is information about how to get it. Even information about where it *isn't* can be helpful. What if you lived your life as a research project for getting what you want and learning what would be best for you?

Learning Experience Nine

Be Here Now

Turn your attention to this moment. And this one. And this one.

Sit quietly by yourself and ask yourself: What is this moment like?

How is this one?

Take time between questions to be with yourself and tune into your senses. See your world. Hear its sounds. Smell its fragrances. Feel its textures.

Feel your own body. Touch your hair, your face. Rest your hands on your thighs; feel the weight of them and their warmth.

What is this very moment like?

Do this for a few minutes. You can also do this with a friend taking turns asking one another: How is this moment? What is this moment like?

Step Ten

Asking for What You Want

In twenty years of working with people, I have seen no skill more valuable for enhancing relationships and getting more of what you want than the simple ability to ask for it. At the same time you probably couldn't count all of the beliefs and judgments about asking for what you want at one sitting. The result leaves us resigned to doing without or resorting to manipulation, coercion, deceit, force, or trying to make people feel bad enough to give us what we want.

A friend who worked in real estate once complained bitterly that a secretary at work referred every call that came in for him to his home number. "I can't even have dinner with friends!" he shouted. "You know once they get you, you can't just hang up on them!"

"Does she know that you'd rather have her take a message?" I asked.

"Oh, I'm sure she knows I'm annoyed," he responded. *It's not the same thing.* Telling someone what you're unhappy about is very different from letting them know what you want.

When we experience disappointment—which so often turns into anger or sorrow—we usually desire something that we aren't expressing, or even allowing in the privacy of our own being. You may want something from yourself, God, the universe, your friends or co-workers. It may be something for yourself or for someone else or something that would benefit the planet. We lose touch with that desire and get lost in anger and resentment or despair about *not* getting what we want.

Desire, or wanting, is such a misunderstood phenomenon. The dictionary defines "to want" as "to lack." And, of course, an abiding awareness of what you lack will soon lead to an image of life that is bleak to behold, indeed. A different experience occurs when you know what you welcome into your life, what you would like to move toward or attract to you. That awareness functions as the inner sense of direction that I mentioned before.

Asking for what you want can be one of the most intimate things that one person can communicate to another. Rather than waiting until you're in pain, or raging inside with the injustice of it all, ask yourself what do you welcome into your life now? Who would you like to have know that?

If you can express your desires as a gift of self-revelation rather than a demand, people can share them with you in a whole new way. Even if they don't want to give you what you want, they may still be on your side and want you to have it. They may even be willing to help you get it.

Many people have become so unaccustomed to asking for what they want and so uncomfortable about it that they will only venture a request after building a firm case for their position, usually *against* somebody else. To prepare a well-documented case before asking for what you want demonstrates an assumption that the other person won't want you to have it. It judges your friend as less than generous and treats him accordingly. A presentation like that usually bumps up against a defensive counter suit. The battle seems to validate the thinking that created the adversarial presentation of the request in the first place.

I'm convinced that most people believe that even God is stingy. You may not ever have heard anyone come right out and say that he believes that God is stingy, but there's a way you can tell if you harbor such a notion. Notice if you pray for less than you really want. Why would you ask for less than you want from a generous source of unlimited abundance?

Tips for Getting What You Want

1. Trust your wanting as an inner sense of direction that will guide you.

2. Share what you want as information about yourself.

3. See the universe as abundant. It is.

4. When you are tempted to demonstrate unhappiness ask yourself what you are wanting. What do you welcome into your life?

5. Don't get hung up on the form. What you really want is probably happiness.

6. Be open to better than you ever imagined.

7. Remember that others are probably doing the best they can with what they know and what they believe so far. That will affect what they want for you. The same is true for you.

8. Live your life as a research project leading to the perfect unfolding of you.

Learning Experience Ten

Blue Sky List

Take a piece of paper and write "Blue Sky List" at the top.

Regard the universe in all it's abundance of form and creativity. If you could get it out of the clear blue sky, without having to do anything for it, what would you want? You don't have to prove you deserve it or know how to pull it off, you just have to know what you welcome into your life.

Write a "Blue Sky List" of what you welcome into your life.

Step Eleven

Why You Want What You Want

Remember the young opera singer who waited on tables in order to support herself? I once asked her why she wanted to sing opera.

After she looked at me as if I were really stupid for a moment, she replied with all the dignity of her calling, "I have a voice that is a gift from God and I'm using it to ask people how they like their soup!"

These questions and answers followed:

Q. "And why, if you have a voice that is a gift from God, do you want to sing Opera?"

A. "Because it would be a crime to waste it."

Q. "Why do you want to avoid wasting it?"

A. "Because I want to use it. I want to share it with people."

Q. "Why do you want to share it with people?"

A. "Because it's beautiful."

Q. "Why do you want to share something beautiful with people?"

A. "Because then I'll be doing what I'm supposed to be doing. I'll be doing what I'm here for."

Q. "Why do you want to be doing what you're here for?"

A. "Because then maybe I could be happy." Her eyes filled with tears and she laughed. "You mean to tell me," she said placing broad, humorous emphasis in each word, "that I have been making myself miserable for years, because I want to be happy? Ohhh, my God!"

I have asked hundreds of people, "Why do you want what you want?" and, "What do you want that for?" Their answers create the perfect definition of happiness in all of it's wonderful forms. They say things like:

To find peace

To feel at one with God and the universe

To feel good

To know I'm doing the right thing

Bliss

Ecstasy

Joy

To be true to myself

To feel love

To have fun

To feel free

To know that I'm okay

To relax

To unfold who I am

To be happy

So often we become unhappy if we don't yet have something we want. We get so lost in the feelings of frustration, anger, shame and despair that we completely forget what we want, what we welcome into our lives. At that moment we stop actively wanting what we want. We make ourselves miserable in order to get what we want so that we can then be happy. That approach to motivation is not only self-defeating, it will get you to be unhappy in order to be happy. That's as close to crazy as I want to get.

Knowing what you want and what you really want it for is the best way I know to greet a brand new day. It allows you to live in the moment, which is the only one you have. You can stop looking at the map, and over your shoulder. You can travel lighter. It's as good for you as sunshine.

Learning Experience Eleven

The Why With the Want

Choose something from your Blue Sky list.

If there's something that you're unhappy about not having, that would be a good one.

Ask yourself: Why do I want that? Or, what do I want that for?

When you get your answer, ask again: Why do I want that?

Ask again and again.

Take each answer and ask yourself: Why do I want that? Or what do I want that for? until you come to the end of your answers.

You'll know you've reached the end when there isn't anything beyond, "I just do." Again, this is not an inquisition or intended to challenge what you want. The purpose is to find out more about how come you want what you want.

Step Twelve

No Fault Living

Perhaps we do everything we do in an attempt to help ourselves and others to live as best we can. We get confused though, and there is so much to learn.

One of the most self-defeating tangles of beliefs that humans have adopted is their faith in the effectiveness of punishment. The failure of punitive action to produce beneficial change reveals itself in the violence committed by people whose parents abused them when they were children. We see it also in the results provided by our prison system. How often does an inmate see the error of his ways and complete his sentence to leave full of high hopes, better able to cope with life in this world and ready to contribute to society?

A friend and former student of mine, Anne Grete Mazziotta, worked as a counselor in a women's prison in Maryland. Most of the inmates were there because they couldn't handle basic life. They had never learned how to accomplish the fundamentals such as:

Finish school.

File your income tax.

Pay your traffic tickets now, or it'll get worse.

Show up at work every day.

Tell the truth most of the time, or at least if you're certain to get caught in a lie.

That absence of basic training got them into trouble. That trouble landed them in prison, for selling drugs or prostituting to support an addiction, for example. When released, they frequently returned to prison for parole violations or minor crimes like shoplifting. These women had never learned to manage schedules, keep appointments, plan ahead, foresee consequences, obey regulations — aspects of life that most people take for granted. They violated the terms of their parole for the same reasons that they didn't hand in their science projects; they never acquired the skills.

The subsequent re-sentencing often added years more to be taken from their lives. The women returned to prison in states of bewildered rage, panic, or depression.

Their anguish and their inability to control the fundamentals of their lives proved heart-wrenching to their counselor. Anne Grete conceived of her new job as trying to find a way to ease the suffering, reduce the stress, and make the time pass as pleasantly as possible. "You know," she said, "your basic, make the best of a bad situation. We did a lot of puzzle therapy, jigsaw puzzles and such."

It didn't take long for Anne Grete to realize that her goal was out of step with the thinking of her colleagues. They placed great faith in the benefits of suffering and punishment. They actually wanted to make the time spent in jail hard, long, and painful. It's unlikely that Anne Grete's colleagues acted differently out of meanness. They genuinely believed, as do most of us, that the best way to get people to change is to make them feel bad. If that doesn't work, make them feel worse. Although the statistics about child abuse and violent crime shock us, the belief in corrective punishment persists.

We humans use that approach more relentlessly on ourselves than any prison guard would. It doesn't work. It seems that you just can't make somebody feel bad enough to be good. We just can't make ourselves feel bad enough to mend our ways. No amount of guilt induces us to give up our old habits or "wicked ways." No amount of self loathing makes us more lovable. Anger at ourselves does not make model citizens of *us* either.

If these things worked we'd live in a crime free world of fully-realized beings with halos. It can't be for lack of trying that they don't work.

The self- defeating faith in the benefits of inflicting pain and suffering colors every area of life. We use it with our children, our mates, co-workers, and students.

This conviction in the power of punishment binds us all to the past with heavy chains. How freeing it might be to take Christ's advice and, "Forgive them, for they know not what they do."

What then is the alternative? Do we simply resign ourselves to less than we want from ourselves and each other? Do we allow criminals free run of the streets? Shall we permit children to harm themselves, each other, or us? Or to treat their parents and teachers with lack of courtesy?

We've relied on induced suffering (from torture chambers to the shaming of a child for wetting his bed) to supply the motivation for change so thoroughly and for so long that we forget how creative we become when we use desire to motivate ourselves and others.

In a world without blame we could move in any direction we choose. We could teach our children about the consequences of their actions without threatening them or harming them or ever wanting them to feel bad or to suffer. We could provide what is lacking rather than seeking to place blame and inflict pain.

An executive for a large computer corporation improved the productivity of several departments dramatically by instituting a new method of conducting meetings. "We will no longer talk about how it got this way, and who's to blame," he announced one day, "I only want to hear about what we can do now to make it better."

There was an elementary school in Manhattan called the Fifteenth Street School. It had very few rules. The students had to attend morning meeting and end of day meeting. They couldn't leave the building on their own until fourth grade. From fourth grade on they had to put a name tag on the "Out" board if they went out for a stroll. They could not interfere with anyone else's ability to learn. The consequences of their own actions became apparent because they were *real*, not because they were enforced.

My son spent most of the first half of first grade in the gym at the Fifteenth Street School. Then he decided he wanted to learn to read. He went to his teacher who set up a time. After about four days, he came home in tears of frustration. "I want to

103

learn how to read," he sobbed, "but it's so hard and so boring." I replied that his teacher wouldn't *make* him do it. "I know," he wailed, "but if I don't come to lessons, she won't either. She said she won't try unless I do!" He learned to read in about three weeks.

Endeavoring to explain this concept at a workshop in New Paltz, New York, I offered the following example of how to teach about consequences without using shame or punishment.

Barnaby and the Storm Drain

As I washed dishes one Fall afternoon, I looked into the mirror before me, over the sink. The mirror provided a pretty view of Joppenberg mountain, just across the street. The sun hit the rocky side with a blaze of gold. I could see the giant concrete pipes stacked by the side of the road awaiting work on the storm drainage system the town was going to install there.

I could also see little Ronnie Schwartzweller's head as he tried to climb out of a large pipe that stood on its end. My eight year old son, Barnaby, and a neighbor kid stuffed Ronnie Schwartzweller, head and all back down into the pipe just as fast as he climbed up and poked it out again. I reacted with horror.

With a total lack of acceptance, I yelled out of the window as only an outraged mother can, "Barnaby, you get in here this minute!"

By the time he had crossed the street, (allowing Ronnie Schwartzweller to escape at will) rounded the corner and come up the walk to the house, I had fortunately remembered something. I remembered what fun it was years ago to lock a city kid that was visiting my neighbors in the barn with our horse. The poor horse was so old all he could do was stand there, but the poor kid from the city didn't know that.

The fun part combined extreme relief that I had escaped an unpleasant spot in the pecking order with the thrill of my first taste of peer power. I grew beyond such sources of excitement by the time I reached ten. Some people never do.

When Barnaby trudged sheepishly into the room, to his great surprise and relief, I said, "I know it's fun, Barn, but you just can't do it." He understood immediately. He said, "I know, Mom." And with a tentative grin admitted, "It really *is* fun though."

This story met with outraged indignation from a local school teacher. First he explained why Barnaby was bad. Then he explained why I was bad. Then he explained why Barnaby should have been punished severely. After a long and patient unravelling of beliefs he asked what led me to think my son had learned the error of his ways. I explained that the kid understood that if he tormented the neighbors the price would be too high. I'd impose sanctions, the neighbor mothers would be all over him and me, the other kids wouldn't like him, he wouldn't like it if the same thing happened to him and so forth and so on.

"Oh!" He exclaimed in gleeful triumph. "You shamed him into capitulation." He simply had no frame of reference to hold the idea that a child could change his behavior simply because he saw a better way.

Notice today how many times you can find a belief in the power of punishment operating in yourself and others. See if you can find alternative ways to motivate yourself and others. Look for opportunities to set a new course *toward* what you want, rather than *away* from what you want to avoid or change.

Several years later, the monster-sewer-stuffer-child spent the summer working at a resort in the Catskill Mountains. He met a man there who was dying from cancer after a long and lonely battle. Barnaby worked an extremely long day as the only dishwasher at the hotel and doubled as bus boy. He spent many of his evenings sitting up late, very late, talking with his friend. He said he mostly listened while the man told about his suffering and the hardships that he faced now as well as in the past. I asked Barnaby if it was painful for him to hear about such difficult challenges and so much pain.

"Not really," he replied, "I'm sorry his life has been like that, but I'm more glad that I can help him by listening."

Many wonderful writers such as Louise Hay and Gerald Jampolsky teach about the real power in forgiveness. In order to forgive, you have to get beyond the desire to correct "wrongs" with punishment. Otherwise you'll be at cross purposes with yourself. You'll try and try to forgive, but it just won't stick.

Find out for yourself, in your own life-laboratory. What might your life be like if for just one day you took a vacation from judgement, blame, recrimination and punishment? Would you stop wanting the best from yourself and others? Would you be more willing to settle for less than your heart's desire? Perhaps the energy that fuels the desire to punish could, if redirected, power creative solutions as yet undreamed of. You may be in for an exciting surprise.

Step Thirteen

Creating New Realities

Did you know that you can do anything "on purpose" to achieve anything? You are in charge of what you do things *for*. You can wash your car for the purpose of balancing your checkbook or in order to meet Mr./Ms. Right. You have total control over what results you desire when you do anything. Take any action and assign a purpose to it. It's more fun and more powerful than "remembering your goals." Did you ever notice how your mind strays and wanders about when you try to visualize on purpose? Every time you designate an intended outcome for an action, you create a living visualization with great impact.

It may be impossible to run a scientific test on how well this method works but you can perform your own lab experiment easily enough. Just pick something you want and assign that outcome as the desired result to all of your activities for a day. Say you want a raise; brush your teeth in order to get a raise that day. Drive your car in order to get a raise that day. Speak to your boss with that purpose in mind. You don't have to ask for the raise. That's not part of the experiment. Eat lunch for that raise. Watch T.V. or work out or daydream after work for that raise. See what the day is like and what happens next.

Choosing the results you desire purposefully will clarify your intent. It will clear your mind and keep you on the path you choose. Purposeful choices strengthen your communication with yourself, with others, and with our higher, more mysterious power, whether you call that power God, the order of the universe, or the way it is.

The essence of communication is intent. Those purposeful choices communicate your intent; it doesn't matter whether your communication is with yourself, your friend, God, or the universe.

Most of the earlier part of this book is intended to help you identify and resolve issues from your past by learning how to unravel the beliefs that keep those issues painfully alive in you. Then we covered ways to help you to tune in to your wanting, to "keep your eye on the prize," (to borrow a powerful phrase from the Civil Rights Movement).

Now we can begin the exciting work of creating a new life, a new reality. Every time a self-defeating belief dissolves in the light of love and insight, a new possibility emerges. If you take action at that point, you breathe life into that possibility.

A student told me about such a creative moment in a love relationship. She and her boyfriend had locked horns in a painful and frustrating argument, filled with anger, fear of loss, confusion and misunderstanding . . . all of the customary ingredients for a fight with a loved one. As she argued, Cora felt a particularly sharp stab of pain followed by a hot flash of rage and a strong desire to inflict pain herself. She managed the following inner dialogue in the heat of battle — no retreat, no surrender intended.

Q. Why do I want to hurt him?

A. Because he hurt me.

Q. What hurts me?

A. He doesn't care. He never did.

111

And there she had it, the belief by the tail. She could then ask herself:

Q. Do I believe that?

A. No, I know he cares. I really do know that he cares.

Cora's anger sort of fizzled at that point. She began to rummage around in the wreckage for a way to find peace. With this new intent the possibility of peace became real and then peace itself did. As the smoke cleared, Cora's boyfriend risked a hesitant question about the recent skirmish.

"When you said I just did that to make you jealous, did you really mean that?"

"No," said Cora, "I just said that because I was mad."

"I'm glad," he breathed in relief, "I wouldn't want anyone to have to feel jealous. I really wouldn't want that for anyone."

"I know," smiled Cora, "I like that about you."

Their new intent to find peace and understanding worked with the ease we attribute to magic. The intent created the opportunity. Cora's boyfriend used that opportunity for clear communication and the intimacy that it leads to when he asked in sincerity, "Did you really mean that?"

Cora and her boyfriend created a new reality in their relationship. They also reshaped their past. It now includes a memory. They remember a painful conflict resolved in honesty, closeness and a deeper sense of friendship. Before the change, a look to the past for information about what to do when having trouble with a boyfriend yielded a different message. It is truly as if they look into a different past every time they add a different event that has a new outcome and new beliefs. That new reality alters their perception of what conflict in close relationships means.

Each moment presents itself with as many choices as there are breaths.

Learning Experience Twelve

Creating a New Reality

Take something from your "Blue Sky List" or something else you'd like to achieve, have, experience.

Write it down.

What are some steps you can take to bring that into reality? Look for things you could enjoy doing to move toward that goal or attract it to you. Let your imagination run wild.

Go over your "Blue Sky List."

For each item on that list ask yourself: Can I have that? Answer yes or no.

For each no answer, ask yourself why? Why can't I have that?

Write down your response. You may have one belief or many.

Ask: Do I believe that?

115

This is a good learning experience to share with a friend or a group for several reasons. One is that since it breaks up your version of reality, it's hard to do. You could use the support. Also the shared insights are truly inspiring.

ⵉ

Step Fourteen

You Can Get There From Here

A wise man once said, "I can predict the future."

"Amazing!" the people cried, "How can you do that?"

"It's easy," he said, "Most likely it will be a continuation of the present."

If you want to change your life, all you have to do is turn, perhaps ever so slightly, and take the very next step in a new direction. It's never, ever, too late to follow your wanting and correct your course as new information becomes available. Bruce Di Marsico, who created the Option Method, once said, "There's a very good view from on top of an obstacle."

To your happiness!

ACKNOWLEDGEMENTS

In grateful appreciation to:

Tori Prinz, Gary Goldman, Dennis Clark and Alice Bruce — the first courageous explorers to take the "Beyond the Past" workshop — and to everyone who followed.

Marty Robertson for reading this and for loving support as I confronted issues from my past.

The ACA Program

Ilona Simon Muller and Anne Grete Mazziotta

Rev. Nancy Anderson, Rev. Carol Carnes, Douglas Wilson, Prue Berry and Deborah Lally, early sponsors of the "Beyond the Past Workshop."

Kati Bower, desktop publisher; her patience matches her perfection.

Rich Mould, Barbara Alba and Ann Epner

Terry Parker, longtime friend and research whiz!

RESOURCES

The following information is intended to share sources of information and inspiration that have enriched my life and helped me to travel more freely.

Adult Children of Alcoholics, sometimes called ACA or ACOA, is listed in the phone book in larger communities. Meetings are free and demand no religious affiliation. If you have difficulty locating meetings in your area try Alcoholics Anonymous, AA, for information.

The Rowe Camp and Conference Center
Kings Highway Road
Rowe, MA 01367   (413) 339-4216

They offer a wonderful array of weekend and week long adventures with gifted seminar leaders in one of the most healing environments you can imagine. The cost is low and the food is great. Write for their catalogue.

The Option Method offers a profoundly useful tool for self exploration. Created by Dr. Bruce Di Marsico, its simplicity is matched by its power. I urge anyone who wants to lead a happier, more creative life to learn how to use Option to unravel the beliefs that choke the life out of us and bind us to the past.

Some books about Option are:

Giant Steps by Barry Neil Kaufman

Emotional Options by Mandy Evans (see order form in the back of this book.)

The support of friends and fellow travellers. Form your own group. One of the most healing and growth provoking experiences of my life was participating in a peer group that lasted two years. I later helped to develop a group of support teams for displaced homemakers in Ulster County, New York. It was a joy to see group after group of women create their own support systems and move into new lives against big odds, if you believe in circumstances! *Travelling Free* is designed to be used by a study/support group as well as by individuals.

ABOUT THE AUTHOR

Mandy Evans was born in Rockville, MD. She studied for the theatre and worked in New York City before training to be a group counselor. She draws on over twenty years of experience using the Option Method. She has worked with thousands of people to free themselves from the beliefs that cause emotional conflict or limit their lives in some way.

FOR INFORMATION ABOUT THE "BEYOND THE PAST WORKSHOP"

Please Contact:

MANDY EVANS
c/o YES YOU CAN PRESS
1106 Second Street, Suite 331
Encinitas, California 92024
(619) 944-6028

ORDER FORM

Satisfaction Guaranteed

Please send me:

❏ EMOTIONAL OPTIONS—How to Use the Option Method. A power packed little book that opens the doors to emotional freedom.
ISBN 1-878639-D3-X $5.95

❏ TRAVELLING FREE—How to Recover from the Past by Changing Your Beliefs. Filled with workshop tested exercises and insights. Compatible with Twelve Step programs.
ISBN 1-878639-04-8 $9.95

❏ CHOOSING HAPPINESS—Mandy Evans at Interface. A funny, insightful audio cassette offers a complete introduction to Option with moving examples of how it works. $8.95

❏ FREE—TOP 20 SELF-DEFEATING BELIEFS—And how to defeat them

Name _____
Address _____
City_____State_____Zip _____

Shipping/handling: $2.50 for the first item and $1.00 for each additional item. (First class mail) Please add 7.25% sales tax for California shipments.

Amount Enclosed _____

Mail check or money order to:

Yes You Can Press
1106 Second Street #331 • Encinitas, CA 92024
(619) 944-6028

TO YOUR HAPPINESS!

Real Life Financial Planning for the New Physician

A Resident's, Fellow's, and Young Physician's Guide to Financial Security

3rd EDITION

Marshall W. Gifford, ChFC, CLU
Todd D. Bramson, CFP®, ChFC, CLU

ASPATORE

Mat # 40906414

ISBN 978-0-314-91631-0

For corrections, updates, comments, or any other inquiries please e-mail
TLR.AspatoreEditorial@thomson.com.

First Printing, 2005
10 9 8 7 6 5 4 3 2 1

ASPATORE

Aspatore Books, a Thomson Reuters business, exclusively publishes C-Level executives (CEO, CFO, CTO, CMO, Partner) from the world's most respected companies and law firms. C-Level Business Intelligence™, as conceptualized and developed by Aspatore Books, provides professionals of all levels with proven business intelligence from industry insiders—direct and unfiltered insight from those who know it best—as opposed to third-party accounts offered by unknown authors and analysts. Aspatore Books is committed to publishing an innovative line of business and legal books, those which lay forth principles and offer insights that, when employed, can have a direct financial impact on the reader's business objectives, whatever they may be. In essence, Aspatore publishes critical tools for all business professionals.

Additional books in the *Real Life* book series

Real Life Financial Planning
(second printing)

Real Life Financial Planning for Young Dentists
(second printing)

Real Life Financial Planning for the High Income Specialist

Real Life Financial Planning for Young Lawyers

Real Life Financial Planning with Case Studies
(second printing)

Real Life Financial Planning with Case Studies
(featuring Langdon Ford Financial)

Real Life Money Management for Pharmacists

Real Life Financial Planning for the Medical Professional

Real Life Financial Planning with Case Studies for Women

Dedications

This book is dedicated to my entire family, especially my wife Tari, who has supported me while I built my practice and provides support on a daily basis. Also, I thank my parents, who taught me that "anything is possible if you have confidence in yourself." I would also like to dedicate this to my clients, who have trusted me and helped me gain the knowledge included in this book.

Marshall W. Gifford

This book is dedicated to my immediate family. Without the love, support, and guidance of all of them, I wouldn't have learned the most important lesson of life. That is, "When all is said and done, it is the quality and depth of relationships and experiences that are the essence of life...not the accumulation of material possessions."

Todd D. Bramson

Thank You

We extend a special thank-you to...
...our clients, who have trusted us with their financial decisions
...our staff, specifically Somer Mansur, Greg Halat, and Michelle Muthiani
...our partners Brett VanderBloemen, Justin Dering, Greg Wikelius, Brian Hensen, Josh Evenson, Jon Ylinen, Ryan Keshemberg, and Jeff Turton
...our business associates, who make work a pleasure

Background and Motivation

I grew up in a small town in Northeast Iowa. My parents were both successful business owners. My father ran an insurance agency, and my mother ran an antique and gift shop. It wasn't until 1989, during my senior year of high school, that I learned how quickly life can change. In February of 1989, I was diagnosed with Lupus Nephritis, a disease of the autoimmune system. In the middle of basketball season and recruiting trips, my season ended. At 6' 4," my weight dropped to 126 pounds. The next seven months I spent in and out of hospitals. I was very fortunate to fully recover physically in late 1989, and have been healthy for the past fifteen years. The experience, however, will never be forgotten. It serves as a reminder to make sure I take care of those closest to me and live every day, because you never know when life will deviate from your plan.

Marshall W. Gifford

I have gained wisdom, strength of character, integrity, empathy, and the value of giving by my parents' example. Unfortunately, my father passed away very suddenly at the age of forty-five, when I was just sixteen. It was only three weeks from the day he discovered a few black and blue marks on his arms to the day he died of acute leukemia. In this short time, we never had a chance to talk about the future, although I feel his guidance through my conscience and in the wisdom of others, including my mother.

It is interesting how the experiences of childhood, both good and bad, mold the path we follow as adults. My dad did not have much life insurance, or any established relationships with trusted advisors. When he died, my mother was lost financially. She was given very poor financial advice, and the small amount of life insurance she had was lost in an unsuitable and inappropriate investment. My family's misfortune defined my passion. It was through this unfortunate situation that I became empowered. My mission has remained intact for more than thirty years, as I decided this would never happen to my family or anyone who entrusted me with their important financial decisions.

Todd D. Bramson

The title of this book is *Real Life Financial Planning for the New Physician*. We do not live life in a controlled environment. The best you can do is plan thoughtfully and thoroughly, factoring in all the potential outcomes.

We would like to share a proverb containing some valuable wisdom and insight:

> *He (or she) who knows, and knows he knows, is wise;*
> **Follow him.**
> *He who knows, but knows not that he knows, is asleep;*
> **Awaken him.**
> *He who knows not, and knows he does not know, is simple;*
> **Teach him.**
> *He who knows not, but does not know that he knows not, is dangerous;*
> **Avoid him.**

We believe it is our mission in life to listen to and learn from, or **follow**, those who fall into the first category. But it is also our mission to take our unique gifts and make them available to those who are asleep or simple by **awakening** and **teaching** them. Also, time is too precious to spend with those who are dangerous. **Avoid** and minimize the amount of time you spend with people who fall into this category, and your enjoyment of life will multiply. We all have unique gifts and abilities, and to the extent that our lives overlap and intertwine, we can all grow together carrying out our unique visions.

It is our hope that this book will educate and motivate you to achieve all of your personal and financial goals.

Marshall W. Gifford and Todd D. Bramson

Real Life Financial Planning
for the New Physician

CONTENTS

1

Introduction

Why the title, *Real Life Financial Planning for the New Physician?*

Quite simply, residents, fellows, and young physicians have unique financial needs. You have so many financial issues and options on a personal and business level. This complexity can make decision-making very difficult. With our thirty years of combined experience catering to the medical profession, we have not seen a resource like this book.

Our experience reveals that most physicians have a significant interest in financial issues, but many are simply too busy to take the time to learn what they need to know. During school, residency, and/or fellowship, the focus is on your training, and few curriculums teach financial planning. There may be a class on practice management or contracts, but none that really address the actual details of a financial plan for you or your practice.

Upon completion of training, your time is spent getting established in a practice. In addition, many of you will get married and start a family, which can delay financial planning even longer. Before you know it, years have gone by and still...no financial plan.

If you have a comprehensive plan, congratulations. This book can serve as a reference to reinforce what you are doing. But like high cholesterol that can't be ignored, you must begin immediately to initiate your financial plan. This book will give you the start you need.

There is so much information "out there," but sometimes not much wisdom. This book summarizes the wisdom we have gained and shared with our clients in individual meetings throughout the years. *Real Life Financial Planning for the New Physician* is simply a practical method of understanding, organizing, and prioritizing financial decisions.

Most financial planning publications, and financial plans themselves, assume everyone lives a long, healthy life and saves a good portion of their income in quality investments that always do well. This book addresses the issues that happen in **real life**, good and bad.

A solid financial plan should make your life simpler by letting you focus on the issues you excel at and enjoy. This may include practicing medicine, spending time with your family, or pursuing hobbies. These activities are more enjoyable knowing that your finances are in order. We hope you take the time to read this book and work with a trained professional to develop and implement a financial plan that meets *your* goals and objectives.

As a young physician, you wear many hats, especially if you are self-employed or a partner in a practice. With that in mind, surrounding yourself with advisors that can help you is crucial to your success. We recommend you have the following specialists on your team:

Financial Advisor – Your financial advisor is often the quarterback of the entire team. They can help organize and prioritize all of your goals and objectives, both business and personal. A comprehensive plan is developed, which coordinates your risk management, savings, retirement, debt management, and tax reduction needs.

Banker – The banker's role will be to arrange financing for buying a private practice. A banker can also help you finance a new building or surgical center, and the necessary equipment. The banker will also help determine the most favorable loan terms. On a personal level, the banker can help with loan consolidations and mortgage financing, as well as cash management accounts.

Attorney – Initially, an attorney may help you review your contract. Then when you buy a house, an attorney should review those documents. Along the way, an attorney will help you draft legal documents such as wills and trusts. As your net worth grows, select an attorney who is an expert in asset protection strategies specific to the state you live in.

Accountant – An accountant will not only make sure you are properly filing your tax returns, but he or she may also assist you in setting up bookkeeping systems, practice valuation, compensation formulas, and payroll services, as well as depreciating and expensing equipment if you have your own practice.

Financial success isn't, as most people might suspect, the ability to make one or two decisions that turn a buck into a million. Rather, financial success is the result of many small but sound decisions that, when compounded, add up to substantial financial security.

You are in complete control...or at least you should be. When it comes to spending and saving, investing and paying taxes, many may offer good advice, but you're the only one who can do anything about it. Maybe you're unsure of your investment options and how to prioritize them. Maybe you don't have a clue where your paycheck goes each month. In any case, if you're reading this book, you already understand the importance of getting your future under control, and that's the crucial first step to financial freedom.

Financial independence and the accumulation of wealth are no accident. Granted, it's not possible to plan for every single event in life, but even tragedy can feel more manageable when you are financially prepared for it. *Many people spend more time planning for a family vacation than for their financial future!* Whether it's preparing for the future, planning for the transition of your business, insuring your family against tragedy, or planning for the good times, your money deserves your undivided attention.

Car accidents, marriage, divorce, children, changing practices, death, retirement, and taxes, for better or worse, are the realities of life. Planning for any circumstance, both happy and sad, may seem like a burden right now, but the proper planning will rescue you when (not if) unforeseen circumstances arise.

The truth is we all need to plan for our financial futures. The question is not whether to plan, but how to go about making a plan, and whether you need a professional to help.

Also, the information age has intensified the field of financial planning. It is interesting to consider that twenty years ago, financial news may have made top headlines two or three times throughout the year when the stock market would do particularly poorly or well, or if there was some other major economic news. Today, however, we have news programs dedicated to nothing else twenty-four hours a day, seven days week, and the number of financial headlines in the daily papers can be overwhelming. Still, there is a big difference between information and wisdom, and that's where the insight of a trusted professional can help.

Should You Hire a Financial Planner?

Several situations that may call for a financial planner's expertise are:

- *You are very busy without much spare time.* In this case, a financial planner can save you a bit of your most precious commodity—time.

- *You are easily bored or overwhelmed by financial questions.* If, for example, preparing a budget is such a nuisance that you can't even imagine having to sort through anything more complex, then hiring a financial planner may be money well spent for greater peace of mind.

- *You are considering a complicated set of employee benefits in combination with personally owned insurance and investments.* You don't want your new benefits to conflict or overlap with your current investments and insurance. A careful review will avoid gaps and/or duplication.

- *You have recently graduated from school and started your residency, or just finished a residency and are suddenly expected to manage a much higher income.* The saying "An ounce of prevention is worth a pound of cure" is an important one in the world of financial planning. Seemingly insurmountable debt plagues the future of many young physicians. Learning whether you should consolidate your student loans, budgeting properly, choosing insurance options, and making wise investments are necessary life skills. Getting professional advice **now** beats paying for costly mistakes later.

- *You are self-employed.* In this case, you most likely have to "wear many hats" as an entrepreneur. You are the physician, the marketer, the practice manager, and probably don't have time to investigate or be aware of the many planning options available to you and your employees. A financial planner can help you sort through the many issues facing you.

The topic doesn't matter, whether it's religion, politics, stocks, insurance, sales loads, or how to finance your house, just to name a few. There are always many individual considerations, and the correct solution depends on a variety of factors. We get leery of advice that suggests you should "always" do this or "never" do that. We believe life, as well as most financial decisions, is more gray than black or white.

We are not the first to say this, and we certainly won't be the last: "It is crucial to trust your own judgment and instinct before taking action, no matter how good someone makes their argument." The best way to gain confidence in your own judgment is to educate yourself on the topic at hand.

Have you thought about any of the following questions?

- How much money should I have in emergency reserves?
- Should I consolidate my student loans?
- In which order should I go about paying off my debt?
- What is the right kind of insurance for me, and how much do I need?
- What insurance should I have for my practice?
- How should I go about setting up a savings plan?
- What are my investment options?

- What is the best type of retirement plan for me and my employees?
- How should I plan for college education for my children?
- How much do I need to save to retire?
- How do I protect my assets in the event of a lawsuit?
- What tax-sheltered options are available to me?
- How do I establish a budget?
- What are the most common financial mistakes people make?

If you don't know the answers, just keep reading, because you're about to find out.

As a medical professional, you face significant transitions. At each one, it is critical that you take the appropriate steps. The major transitions for all physicians are from medical school to residency, and from residency to practice. The third key transition facing some is becoming a partner in a practice. Each of these transitions poses its own unique challenges, and planning opportunities.

We will discuss all these issues in more detail throughout the book, but to summarize, as you transition from medical school to residency, the key issues to address are:

- Consolidate your student loans to lock in your interest rate, and/or simplify the management of them.
- Fund a Roth IRA if cash flow allows. You may be unable to fund it once you enter practice due to the income restrictions on the Roth IRA.
- Purchase an individual occupation-specific disability policy to protect yourself and your family in the event of a disability. Most training programs offer group disability of 60 to 80 percent of your salary, which is not enough to cover your loan payments and house or rent payments. It is imperative that if you are unable to work that you are still able to make your payments and still have money left to live.

- Obtain an inexpensive convertible term life policy to protect your family and your insurability. The cost is normally around $30 to $50 per month per $1 million of coverage.
- Consider purchasing a home if your program is longer than three years.
- Purchase an umbrella liability policy of at least $1 million to protect your assets against lawsuits arising from personal negligence or the acts of others. The cost of this is normally $100 to $150 **per year**. As your net worth increases, raise your umbrella liability coverage to the maximum you can get.
- Draft a will and appoint guardians and trustees if you have minor children.

The goal in residency or fellowship is to guard against catastrophic financial problems, protect your insurability, initiate a basic savings program, and educate yourself so you can become financially independent as efficiently as possible once you enter practice.

At the conclusion of residency or fellowship, the key issues to address are:

- Set your financial parameters and determine your key financial goals.
- Implement a plan with your increased income to accomplish your financial goals.
- Allocate at least 20 percent of your income to debt reduction or asset accumulation.
- Begin contributions to pre-tax retirement plans such as 401(k)s, 403(b)s, 457 plans, or other qualified plans through your practice.
- Increase your disability insurance.
- Review your life insurance to make sure it is maximized.
- Establish an asset protection plan.
- Establish a debt reduction strategy.

Each time you receive a significant raise, make sure you set a portion aside for your financial priorities. If you save 20 percent or more of your income, you should be financially independent within twenty-five years under most circumstances. Getting in the habit of saving early is much easier than adjusting to your new income and then trying to cut expenses in the future. At your age, it is important to periodically review your goals to make sure you are still on track. We suggest that once or twice a year is normally sufficient.

2

Where Do I Start?

Your Net Worth Statement

The starting point of any financial plan is to calculate your current net worth. This is a snapshot of what you are worth at an exact point in time. To determine your net worth, you simply add up all of your assets and subtract all of your liabilities (debts). Often, when you are just starting out, the net worth is actually a negative number, because the liabilities exceed the assets.

To measure your financial progress, it is important to know your net worth. Many people measure their financial progress by how much money they have in the bank. In reality, as the value of your assets go up, such as a house, business, or investments, and as you pay debts down, your net worth may be increasing more dramatically than you think. The most important way to measure financial progress is to calculate your net worth regularly. After you learn how to do it once, it will be easy.

In simple terms, what would you be worth if you sold everything you owned and turned it into cash, then paid off all your debts? If this is the first time you're preparing a net worth statement, it's also a good idea to try to estimate what you think your net worth has been over the last few years. Hopefully you will be pleasantly surprised at the progress you've made.

There are several categories within the net worth statement.

Fixed assets is the first category, and includes those assets that do not have a risk of a loss of principal. These include very conservative assets. A few examples would be checking and savings accounts, money market funds, certificates of deposit, T-bills, EE savings bonds, and whole life insurance cash values. These would be assets you have access to in an emergency, and they are available now, so they are considered liquid.

Variable assets include most other financial assets. Examples include stocks, bonds, mutual funds, retirement plans, or any investment where the principal can fluctuate.

Your personal and/or other assets would include tangible assets such as your house, personal or business property, and vehicles. Other tangible assets, such as a boat, computer, and camera, would also be included here.

Don't get too bogged down trying to establish a value for every piece of personal property. You may already have that information available from your homeowner's or renter's insurance policies, but if not, a rough estimate will work just fine. The main reason for gathering this information is to have an estimate so you can monitor trends. This way, when you are reviewing your net worth after some time, you will be able to track how this category has changed or account for some of the money you spent.

*Tip: Use a video camera to film each room in your house, including closets and the garage. In the event of a loss, it will be much easier to remember for the insurance company's reporting purposes.

Fixed Assets:
    Savings Account: $15,000
    Checking Account: $3,000
    Certificate of Deposit: $2,000
    Total: **$20,000**

Variable Assets:
    IRA: $13,000
    Roth IRA: $9,000
    Mutual Funds: $10,000
    Individual Stocks: $2,000
    Variable Life Cash Value: $4,000
    401(k) Balance: $40,000
    Total: **$78,000**

Personal and Other Assets:
    Home: $375,000
    Vehicle: $20,000
    Personal Property: $30,000
    Total: **$425,000**

Total Assets: **$523,000**

Liabilities:
    Mortgage: $290,000
    Home Equity Line: $35,000
    Vehicle Loan: $10,000
    Credit Cards: $2,000
    Student Loans: $110,000
    Total: **$447,000**

Net Worth (Assets Minus Liabilities):   **$76,000**

For your *liabilities*, list the amount you would owe if you could pay off the amount today, not the total of the payments over time, which includes interest. Don't forget to include all loans like mortgages, auto loans, credit cards, student loans, personal debts, and consumer loans.

Subtract your total liabilities from your assets to arrive at your net worth. For many people, this can be a sobering experience. Keep in mind that it is typical for new physicians to have a negative net worth due to substantial student loans. However, your education is an investment in your financial future. Where else could you have invested $150,000 and expect a return of $100,000+ each year for the next thirty years?

If your net worth is negative, your first financial goal is to get your net worth back to zero. This can be done by reducing debt or accumulating assets. For you, it is especially important to establish a financial plan and get control of your financial life as soon as possible.

The Millionaire Next Door, by Thomas Stanley, outlines some benchmark figures for what your net worth should be at any given time, age, or stage in life. Your net worth represents your financial security and, ultimately, financial independence. So, of course, the closer you are to retirement, the higher your net worth should be. A successful financial plan achieves one's maximum net worth, works under all circumstances, and optimizes the enjoyment of your wealth. It will also be important to insure yourself against unforeseen tragedies and to consider whether you want to leave an inheritance to your family or your favorite charity, establishing a legacy that lives on after you.

In summary, the most critical starting point to a financial plan is evaluating your net worth. Then, on a periodic basis, you can compare the results in order to establish trends and measure improvement. A convenient time to do this is once a year when you're doing your taxes. This way, all the paperwork is readily available and you're focused on your annual earnings and expenditures. Keep all the financial records together from each year's tax forms and net worth calculations for easy reference.

Your Budget

After calculating your net worth, look at your monthly expenses and determine where your money is being spent.

For most people, the thought of budgeting is painful. In our opinion, the benefits of having a successful financial future outweigh the frustrating budgeting process. It is very important to know, generally, where your money goes. It is helpful to track expenses to see if there are inefficiencies in your business or personal habits or hobbies that cost more than you think.

Any successful financial plan requires an understanding of your cash flow so you can establish systematic savings to retirement funds, college funds, debt payoffs, or emergency funds. We have found that if you set up an automated savings of 70 to 80 percent of your surplus cash flow, your household finances should function smoothly. The example below assumes an income of around $210,000. Obviously, during your training, your income will not be as high. Most residents and fellows take home between $2,000 and $2,800 per month, depending on your year in the program.

Example:

Monthly after-tax income:	$12,000
Monthly expenses:	$8,000
Surplus:	$4,000

It should be easy to save $3,000 per month automatically (75 percent of $4,000 = $2,800).

To determine your surplus, it is helpful to track your income and expenses for a couple of months.

Sample Budget

Net Income after Taxes:	$_____

subtract

Mortgage or Rent:	$_____
Car Payment:	$_____
Student Loans:	$_____
Groceries:	$_____
Travel:	$_____
Entertainment/Meals Out:	$_____
Insurances:	$_____
Utilities:	$_____
Phones:	$_____
Clothing:	$_____
Child Care:	$_____
Health Care:	$_____
Internet:	$_____
Gifts:	$_____
Dues:	$_____
Charitable Contributions:	$_____
Miscellaneous:	$_____
This remainder equals your surplus:	$_____

Many people overlook the miscellaneous expenses. These expenses individually are not significant, but added together can be quite large. Examples of these are home repairs, veterinary bills, haircuts, clothing, oil changes, car repairs, household items, lunches out, coffee, diapers, and so on. To get a good idea of your miscellaneous expenses, you may want to carry around a pocket calendar for a month or two and write down the money you spend.

Once you have a good idea what your monthly inflows and outflows are, automate your savings. Treat your investment amount as a bill you pay every month. Our experience shows that if you don't get in the habit of saving money on a regular basis, either through a payroll deduction or an automatic withdrawal from your checking account, the money you intended to go toward savings or investments is simply spent elsewhere. Initially, it is not the amount being saved that is important, but the habit being formed.

The following chart illustrates the importance of developing the habit of saving as soon as you can. The monthly savings amount is what would be needed to be saved starting at that age to accumulate $1,000,000 by age sixty-five at 8 and 10 percent net rates of return.

Age	Monthly Savings Amount	
	10%	8%
25	$158	$287
35	$492	$671
45	$1,316	$1,698
55	$4,882	$5,467

To further demonstrate the importance of the compounding of capital over time, here is the result of saving $10,000 per year at 9 percent into a tax-deferred account:

Age to Start	Account Balance at Age 65
25	$3,682,918
35	$ 1,485,752
45	$557,645
55	$165,602

Both tables illustrate the power of compound interest. Even small amounts early in life can have a huge impact on your retirement account balances. We strongly recommend that as you transition from school to your practice, you immediately set some important financial goals. Write down what is important to you. This could be retiring at age fifty-five, paying off school loans by age thirty-five, funding college for two children, owning a practice in three years, or having a second home in ten years. Determine what type of financial commitment those goals require, and establish the appropriate investment accounts for your goals.

Generally speaking, if you start saving in your late twenties, a savings rate of 15 percent of your gross income should be enough to keep you safe from financial worries at retirement. If you are getting a later start in your mid-thirties, you may need to be saving 20 to 25 percent. If you have accounted for your long-term financial security, it makes spending the remainder more rewarding by eliminating the guilt or fear many people feel in their day-to-day finances, or when making large purchases.

3

The Pyramid

If you took a jigsaw puzzle and dumped all the pieces on the table, it is initially a daunting task to begin to put the puzzle together. Grab a puzzle piece out of the pile at random, and it's hard to know where that piece fits into the big picture. It is much easier to put the puzzle together if you have a picture of what the scene will look like once completed. So, you look at the picture on the box to give you a guide to what the puzzle looks like when completed. We designed the pyramid as a method of seeing how a properly designed financial plan looks when it is put together correctly.

The pyramid is a method of explaining the financial planning concept by categorizing your financial plan into stages. Of course, individual goals, habits, accomplishments, and so on are all unique, but most people share the same fundamental life stages. As a method of efficiently organizing your financial life, the pyramid represents the key to financial independence, and demonstrates the basic goal of increasing your assets and reducing your debt in order to have enough money invested to retire comfortably. Individuals may place more or less importance on one section of the pyramid than another, which is perfectly acceptable.

Without a doubt, organizing your finances in order to build a solid base is the first step. If you do not do this, you may be subjecting your financial situation to undue risk, which will cause problems later on. On the other hand, it's also important not to place too much emphasis on only one stage, neglecting the overall balance. This could be a sign of being overly conservative. As an example, not taking advantage of higher-potential returns in equity (stock) or real estate investments may mean losing your purchasing power in the long run, because the dollars may be worth less, due to the effects of taxes and inflation.

It is very important to try to accomplish a lifelong financial balance. You certainly don't want to scrimp all your life and get to the age of sixty-five with a large amount of money saved, only to be in poor health and not be able to enjoy it. By the same token, you don't want to be nearing retirement and realize you haven't saved enough and now must take a substantial drop in your standard of living or continue to practice longer than you wanted to. The ideal situation would be to retire at the same or a greater standard of living than you were accustomed to while practicing, but not feel at any time that you have greatly sacrificed.

A fundamental of short- and long-term financial success is living on less than your income. If you can get used to living on 80 percent of your income, this allows you to commit 20 percent of your income to your net worth. Initially, this may mean aggressively paying off loans, but over time, the majority of this extra income should be saved.

As you can see by the diagram, there are four main stages to the financial planning pyramid: the *Security and Confidence Stage*, the *Capital Accumulation Stage*, the *Tax-Advantaged Stage*, and the *Speculation Stage*.

The ideal investment is completely liquid and has lots of tax advantages, a high rate of return, and low risk. If you find an advisor or salesperson claiming to have such an investment, you would be wise to avoid them, as they are dangerous. This ideal investment does not exist. Let's use an analogy of spinning plates. If you have ever been to a circus or seen a juggler, you may have seen a performer attempt to spin a lot of plates on long sticks—all at the same time. The objective is to take limited energy, and allocate it in such a manner as to keep all the plates spinning. It doesn't do any good to devote a lot of time to one spinning plate while the others are slowing down, wobbling, and falling down. The goal is to keep all the plates spinning.

Pyramid of Financial Needs

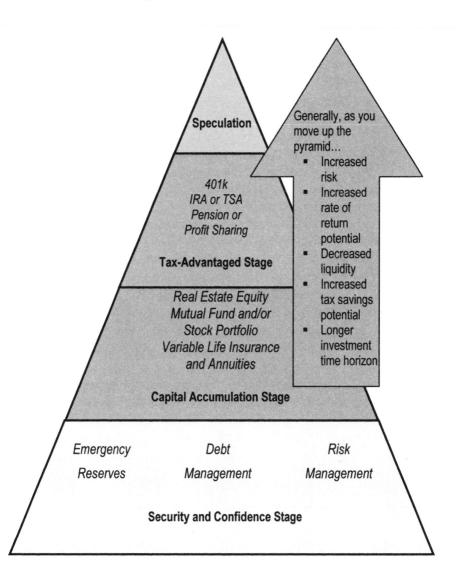

Your financial plan is on somewhat the same level, with each financial decision representing a different plate. First of all, you need to find out which plates you want to start spinning, and then direct your dollars to keep them going. You could have several debt reduction plates, some risk management (insurance) plates, retirement and/or college education plates, and so on. Each individual situation is going to be different. Again, there are limited resources that need to be allocated in such a way as to accomplish all of your goals. This is where the advice of a professional and experienced financial advisor can be very valuable.

The key financial variables in the pyramid are risk, liquidity, rate of return, and tax advantages. The money in your emergency reserves and at the *Security and Confidence Stage* should be very liquid or accessible. Generally, as you move to higher stages in the pyramid, the less liquid your funds become.

Risk and rate of return tend to go hand in hand. The higher the amount of risk you take, the higher the rate of return could potentially be, **given time**. In the pyramid, lower risk with lower rates of return should be at the base of your planning. The risk and the potential rate of return increase as you move up the pyramid. Historically, stock market and investing returns become more predictable the longer the timeframe that is considered. Keep in mind, however, that past performance is not indicative of future results. Investments will fluctuate and, when redeemed, could be worth more or less than when originally invested.

At the lower level of the financial pyramid, there are typically not many tax advantages. If you have money in a savings account, that money is generating ordinary income on which you are paying taxes each year. On the other hand, when you put money into a qualified retirement plan, the contribution is on a before-tax basis, delaying and deferring the tax to a later date. Under most circumstances, however, you cannot touch the money in your qualified plan until age fifty-nine-and-a-half without paying a 10 percent early withdrawal penalty, plus the income taxes due on that amount. The rule of thumb on tax savings is similar to risk and rate of return. As you move up the pyramid, you'll have greater potential tax advantages on your investments.

A Discussion of Risk

There is no such thing as a risk-free investment—even a savings account is not risk-free. Let us explain. Risk is commonly discussed in terms of loss of principal. During the recent bear market (a period of downturn in the stock market), many investors lost some of the value of their investment if they owned stocks, bonds, and/or stock or bond mutual funds. There are other forms of risk besides market risk.

Purchasing Power Risk: With respect to money, risk can be defined as anything that threatens purchasing power. This can occur when an investment declines in value or an investment after taxes and inflation does not equal inflation. If the cost for products and services rises faster than the interest rate being credited on your savings, money market, or checking accounts, you are exposed to purchasing power risk. While you don't lose any principal, you are still losing ground relative to inflation. This is a particular problem currently for retirees or young people who view these savings-type accounts as safe in light of the recent market volatility. If your investments are not earning, after taxes, more than inflation, you are losing money (purchasing power) each year and run a real risk of running out of money.

Interest Rate Risk: Bonds and fixed-income securities are subject to this risk. Your principal value can decline if interest rates climb quickly. The severity of the loss is often magnified by the duration and/or maturity of the bonds and the credit quality. At this time, when interest rates are near forty-year lows, many people who own fixed-income securities are unknowingly subjecting their investments to interest rate risk.

Business Risk: This is the risk of losing money due to circumstances out of your control. A business could go bankrupt, and your investment becomes worthless.

Liquidity Risk: This is the risk associated with being invested in real estate, limited partnerships, businesses, and other investments where there is sometimes no immediate market for your value. This is problematic if you have a need for cash and you cannot sell or liquidate your shares. You would invest in something like this only if you had sufficient assets available besides this investment.

Regulatory Risk: Investors run the risk that government policy decisions or influences of society as a whole could endanger an investment's value. Environmental and tax legislation can have a dramatic impact on certain investment values, up or down. It is important to note this risk when investing.

Currency Risk: An investment in international securities can be affected by foreign exchange rate changes, political and economic instability, as well as differences in accounting standards.

Asset Protection Risk: This is the risk associated with a loss of net worth due to lawsuits, malpractice claims, and so on. The higher your income and net worth is, the greater the risk. The more complex planning goes beyond the scope of this text and includes titling and ownership issues, legal documents, and so on.

Diversity Risk: This will be discussed at length later in the book, but allow us to overstate the obvious: DIVERSIFY!

In summary, a properly structured financial plan will balance all of these variables so that you are diversified by asset class, risk levels, tax treatment, and time horizon.

4

The Security and Confidence Stage: Emergency Funds

This stage is divided into three main sections, with an emphasis on building up emergency reserves, making sure debt is under control, and taking care of risk management (insurance) needs. Each of these factors is equally important. Most people agree on the need to have money accessible for emergencies, to pay their debts, and to be adequately insured. The trick to the individual financial plan is to figure out the appropriate level for each of these.

Emergency Reserves

The one constant in life is that there will always be surprises. The purpose of an emergency reserve fund is just what it sounds like—money that is very accessible when you really need it. The main characteristic of an investment in this category would be the money that is liquid, yet safely invested, so the principal remains intact. The most common mistake people make here is not having adequate reserves or taking undue risk with these funds. This money needs to remain liquid in case of unexpected expenses like car expenses, home repairs, job loss, or medical emergencies. For most people, peace of mind is the main benefit of having an adequate emergency reserve fund. When you are financially prepared for these surprises, they become less stressful and are therefore easier to deal with emotionally.

As a general rule of thumb, your emergency reserve account would be able to cover approximately three months of bills. So, if your monthly expenses are averaging $7,000, your emergency reserve fund should be $21,000. During your residency or fellowship, your expenses may be closer to $2,000 to $4,000 per month, depending on if you are married or single. Ideally, an emergency fund for a single resident would be around $6,000, and for a married couple possibly as high as $12,000. We realize this can be difficult to accumulate given your limited income. This is a rough guide, and you may want to consider having a higher emergency reserve if you anticipate a big purchase, such as a car or home. Ideally, you do not want to deplete your emergency reserve completely in order to purchase such items.

If you are self-employed in your own practice, it is also important to maintain a cushion in your business accounts in the event of an unexpected large expense or your inability to work for a period of time. Business overhead coverage does not begin paying for thirty to sixty days. So keeping two months of your overhead in reserves for your practice is recommended. Until you are able to accumulate this, have a line of credit approved and available to you in order to address short-term cash flow fluctuations.

The typical investments that can be used to hold your emergency reserves would include bank vehicles or money market funds. The common theme among these vehicles is their liquidity and the safety of the principal. If you use a bank for your emergency reserves, typically these funds are in savings accounts and interest-bearing checking accounts, as well as money market funds.

For safety of principal and liquidity, savings accounts are the most common option, but not necessarily the best. Such accounts are insured, so there is no market risk but lots of purchasing power risk. However, this also means there is typically a lower yield than other investments.

Another option is a CD (certificate of deposit) with a relatively short maturity. The disadvantage to a CD is that the money is tied up for a certain length of time, and removing the funds sooner will result in an interest rate penalty. To avoid this problem, it can make sense to stagger your CD maturities so that you always have some that come due every six months or so. Therefore, you can access it if you need to or reinvest it if you don't.

A money market mutual fund is often the best choice as an emergency reserve possibility. Many people incorrectly associate the term "mutual fund" with high risk. However, a mutual fund only has as much risk as the underlying investments it owns. A money market mutual fund pools investors' dollars in the typical mutual fund style, and purchases jumbo CDs through banks, treasury securities (T bills), as well as commercial paper. Most money market funds have a check writing privilege, which allows you to write checks against your account, subject to minimums of usually $250 or $500. The rate of return earned on these funds will fluctuate based on the short-term money market, but is typically competitive with the interest rate at the time. **Investments in a money market fund are neither insured nor guaranteed by the FDIC, or any other government agency. Although the fund seeks to preserve the value of your investment at $1.00 per share, it is possible to lose money by investing in the fund.**

A home equity line of credit is another option. If you have over 20 percent equity in your house, and if interest rates are low and tax-deductible, this option should not be discounted. In fact, in periods of time during a low interest rate environment, maintaining an open line of credit against your house equity is a favorable form of a source of emergency reserve cash. It could also be used to pay down a high-interest credit card or for a major purchase like a car. The drawback is that it needs to be paid off when you sell your house, which of course would result in fewer proceeds at closing. If your house would decline in value, creating less equity, you may have to pay off the home equity line and/or face a higher interest rate on the loan. You could jeopardize your ability to make the mortgage payments, leading to default. While interest rates on home equity loans are higher than a few years ago, this may still be an option worth considering, especially if you can use the money to pay off higher-interest consumer debt. You should never take home equity and invest in the market. This is a dangerous practice that encompasses too much risk.

Life insurance cash values on permanent policies are another source of emergency funds. The returns vary, depending on the type of policy, so work carefully with your advisor to select a policy that fits your objectives. It is usually possible to take out a loan or borrow against your cash value, using it as collateral. Sometimes you can take an outright withdrawal of the money. Remember, though, that any loans or withdrawals taken will reduce both the cash value and death benefit.

5

The Security and Confidence Stage: Debt Management

If you are in the fortunate situation of having no debts, congratulations! If you come from the school of thought that you don't ever want to owe anything to anybody, debt management is not an issue. However, in today's society, this ideology is very uncommon, and many people could use some strategies on effectively managing their debt.

The typical young physician has $100,000 to $250,000 in student loans. In addition, many have a car loan, personal loans, and credit card debt. Make it a priority to pay off all the higher-rate loans (currently those above 8 percent). As of the writing of this book, according to the federal government's student loan Web site, the current federal student loan rates are at 6.8 percent. See www.studentaid.ed.gov for more information. This is a fixed rate and cannot be changed.

If you have other loans from medical school, you can consolidate them, but your interest will be the weighted average of all your loans, so there is little advantage to consolidating aside from having one payment. By consolidating, however, you no longer have the option to strategically eliminate your highest-interest debt and free up cash flow. If you have consolidated, the typical consolidation will fix your interest rate for the next thirty years. Most consolidation programs offer rate reductions of .25 percent for automating your payment, and an additional .5 to 1 percent reduction for successive on-time payments of thirty-six months. In 2001 and 2002, consolidating was an easy decision due to the historically low interest rates.

The interest rate charged on existing non-consolidated federal student loans changes each year on July 1. Effective in 2010, students graduating from medical school will no longer have the option of consolidating due to the new rules, effective July 1, 2006, which fix federal rates on new loans at 6.8 percent.

You can make additional payments to your student loans without penalty to accelerate your debt reduction goals. If you were able to consolidate and lock in your rate at 2 to 5 percent, the main motivation to pay them off is the good feeling of moving toward becoming debt-free. Your net worth, however, can potentially grow faster by paying off higher-interest debt and/or investing at an after-tax rate of greater than the interest rate on your student loans. As rates climb for non-consolidated loans, or if you have higher-rate loans from the 1990s, it may make sense to more aggressively pay off the debt. Working with an experienced financial advisor will be very helpful as you consider all of your options.

Student Loan Management during Residency or Fellowship

When you graduate from medical school, you will receive a six-month grace period on your federal student loans. After those six months, you will either need to begin making payments or file for an economic hardship deferment or forbearance. If your loan balances are low, beginning payments can be a viable option. If you have federal student loan balances in excess of roughly $115,000, you should qualify for economic hardship deferment. However, at the time of the writing of this book, there is legislation pending to eliminate economic hardship altogether and force residents to make income-based repayments. The payments would be based on a formula factoring in your loan balance and your income. For updated information on income-based repayments and the new rules, refer to www.ibrinfo.org. This is an independent source of information regarding the new federal student loan payment and forgiveness programs.

If you are able to get economic hardship deferment, qualification is based on a formula set by the federal government. If you qualify, the federal government will continue to pay the interest on your subsidized loans. Your unsubsidized loans will accrue interest. You can qualify for economic hardship deferment for up to three years. Under the new rules, forbearance will still be an option even if economic hardship is not.

Forbearance does not adversely affect your credit, and must be granted on federal loans during residency or fellowship. While in forbearance, you make no payments, but your subsidized and unsubsidized loans accrue interest. If most of your loans were taken out before 2006, this rule change will not have significant adverse effects, since your interest rates should be very low and you only have a few years left until your training concludes. For those with the majority of their debt at 6.8 percent, forbearance could add a significant amount to your eventual loan balance, because all your debt will accrue interest at 6.8 percent compounded throughout training.

Make sure when you finish a residency and enter a fellowship to clarify your employment status. Many programs consider fellows to be students. If this is the case, you can apply for true deferment again, just like when you were in medical school. To verify this, you will generally need to send a letter to your loan administration company from your program coordinator on the institution's letterhead attesting to your status.

Other Debt Issues

If you have personal debt such as credit cards or high-interest personal loans, you should pay those off quickly, especially if the interest rate is above 10 percent. As each loan is paid off, apply the payment to another loan to accelerate your debt reduction. When all high-interest (greater than 10 percent) loans are paid off, it would be appropriate to begin contributions to 401(k)s, 403(b)s, IRAs, and other investments. If you have debt with an interest rate of 5 percent or lower, you can start saving for other financial goals and making minimum payments on the low-interest debts.

With mortgage debt and business debt, a similar analysis should be applied. However, mortgage and business debt have the additional advantage of being tax-deductible. Student loan interest is subject to adjusted gross income limitations.

When purchasing a home, try not to finance more than two and a half to three times your annual income if you want to be financially independent at an early age. It may be difficult to stay within those parameters during your training. It is acceptable to buy a home that is a larger multiple of your income during this stage. This will allow you to get into the real estate market and away from renting, which is always a significant financial milestone. It is also advantageous to minimize the number of real estate transactions you engage in, because they involve substantial fees, commissions, and transaction costs.

You should also avoid private mortgage insurance, if possible. That can be done with a combination of two loans. One is a traditional mortgage, and the other is held by a bank as a home equity line of credit. Also, consider how long you plan on staying in a home when determining the best financing.

If you plan to be in a home for only five years, you should consider a 5/1 adjustable rate mortgage versus a fixed thirty-year loan. The interest rate will be lower on the 5/1 adjustable rate mortgage, since the lender is only guaranteeing your rate for five years as opposed to thirty, even though both loans are amortized over thirty years. One should note that this strategy is dependent on you selling your house in five years. At year six and beyond, one's monthly payments will increase.

The type of loan you use for your home can also be a function of the asset protection laws of your state. If your state protects the equity in your home from lawsuits, you may want to pay it off in a relatively short period of time and view it as conservative investment. If your state protects very little equity, you may want to use an interest-only loan and direct what would be the principal payment into a protected asset.

In this book, we are discussing issues from a financial perspective, and we realize that there is an emotional aspect to debt as well. Sometimes the emotional dislike and stress of debt can outweigh the benefits of carrying very low-interest debt. In these situations, by all means, pay the loans off and free up your cash flow.

General Debt Guidelines and Information

- Prioritize your debt based on interest rates, and eliminate the loans from the highest to the lowest rate.
- Pay off all debt with rates above 8 percent as soon as possible.
- Once you enter practice, do not finance more than 2.5 to 3 times your annual gross income on your home, if you want to be financially independent at an early age.
- Check your credit report annually. Go to the Web site at www.annualcreditreport.com as a starting point.

It is a good idea to review your credit report every year. The financial information included in this report will have a bearing on whether you can obtain a loan, get auto or home insurance, rent an apartment, or even apply for a job. Contact the credit bureaus and correct any errors you find.

6

The Security and Confidence Stage:
Risk Management and Insurance

Protecting yourself against unforeseen catastrophic losses is the third critical area of the base of the pyramid and the *Security and Confidence Stage*. In fact, think of this as a three-legged stool. Kick one leg out, and the stool will not stand. The financial pyramid is just like that.

Important insurance coverage includes health, auto, disability, life, liability, malpractice, business overhead, disability buyout, long-term care, and homeowner's or renter's. In many cases, life and/or disability insurance are overlooked. However, these can be critically important, depending on your personal situation.

The reason for placing risk management at this point is obvious. You need to protect yourself from losses that would create such a hole that you may otherwise never dig yourself out of. Then, once you are on your way to financial independence, insurance plays an equally important role in protecting your assets.

While you don't want to have any gaps in your insurance protection, you certainly don't want to overlap or duplicate coverage. The ideal financial plan will have you paying reasonable premium levels while providing maximum protection. Remember, the major role of insurance is to protect against catastrophic losses. A common mistake is trying to insure too many contingencies or not using deductibles to your advantage.

You will want to ask yourself a couple of questions before purchasing insurance:

- Is the premium for this coverage going to dramatically affect my lifestyle?
- If I do not buy this coverage and suffer the losses that would have been covered, would I be in grave financial trouble?

If the answer to the first question is "No" and the answer to the second is "Yes," the insurance in question is right for you. If not, reconsider the structure and price of the insurance. Consult an experienced financial professional to help you determine the appropriate levels of coverage and how to structure your insurance within the context of a comprehensive financial plan.

When it comes to life insurance, it is easy to become confused. Some complicated terminology like "term life," "whole life," "universal life," "variable adjustable life," and so on may put you off, but by understanding just a few terms and some of the benefits and disadvantages, you will be much better prepared to evaluate the coverage that is best for you. If structured correctly, life insurance can be one of the most versatile and powerful financial tools available, and should not be overlooked.

Life Insurance

Life insurance has many uses. The simplest need to understand is the need to protect the ones you care about in the event of your untimely death. Additional uses are to:

- Protect your family's financial security
- Secure a loan to buy a practice
- Accumulate and protect wealth (permanent life policies only)
- Pay estate taxes
- Draw more income from your retirement assets without the fear of leaving nothing to your heirs

- Provide liquid dollars in the event of an untimely death of a business partner
- Provide the insured person with peace of mind

Focusing on the simplest need for coverage, which is to protect the ones you care about in the event of your untimely death, it is important to understand how the policy works. Life insurance benefits are stated in a specific lump sum. For example, a $1,000,000 policy would pay $1,000,000 income tax-free to the stated beneficiary upon death of the insured.

Since your income terminates at your death, it would be advisable to provide for a lump sum that would continue an adequate portion of your income to your family. As a hypothetical example, if you make $200,000 annually, and you die tomorrow and want to continue your $200,000 income indefinitely to your family, you will need about $4 million in life insurance. The $4,000,000 would be payable income tax-free to your family. If the lump sum is invested at 5 percent interest, your family could draw $200,000 per year of taxable income without depleting the principal. It is wise to use a conservative investment return on death benefit proceeds, as beneficiaries will most likely be very conservative with managing the insurance money. This simple analysis does not factor in potential Social Security benefits or the long-term effects of inflation.

Life insurance is one of the only insurance coverages that people generally don't think about insuring to full replacement value. If your $500,000 home burned down, would you want it replaced with a $200,000 home? No. If your $200,000 income is lost to your family, do you want to replace it with a $50,000 income, $100,000 income, or full replacement of $200,000? Generally, most people would want to insure for full replacement value. The amount of life insurance you should own is the amount you would buy today if you knew you were going to die tomorrow.

Types of Life Insurance

There are two broad types of life insurance—term and permanent. To understand the difference, it is helpful to compare term insurance to renting an apartment and permanent life insurance to owning a home. Term insurance is inexpensive when you are young, but the cost increases exponentially as you age. You can buy a term policy where the premium goes up every year or stays level for five, ten, twenty, or thirty years. Term insurance provides a large amount of temporary coverage at a low cost for young, healthy people.

The cost for $1,000,000 of term insurance for a twenty-five- to thirty-five-year-old is relatively inexpensive, so protecting you and your family is quite affordable. Your term policy should be convertible to a permanent policy without medical underwriting. This guarantees that if your health changes, you do not need to worry about re-qualifying for the coverage after the initial term. So, be sure the company you purchase your term insurance with has a competitive permanent policy to convert to.

As a long-term strategy, some advisors recommend buying term insurance and taking the difference in premiums between the term and permanent policy and investing it. This can be an effective strategy if you have the discipline to invest the difference on a monthly basis, and are sure you will not want life insurance later in life. Keep in mind that over the course of twenty or more years, the tax implications of this strategy, if invested in non-qualified accounts, can become significant. The tax inefficiencies increase as you near retirement.

These inefficiencies can be magnified when you reallocate your portfolio to become more conservative as you get older. This may require owning more bonds. To accomplish this, you must pay capital gains taxes when you sell your stock portfolio to buy bonds. Bonds also generate ordinary income, which for highly compensated physicians will be at a higher tax rate than the current capital gain and dividend distributions from your stock portfolio. Taxes are owed annually on this strategy, because most physicians will have exhausted their tax-deferred investment options such as 401(k)s, IRAs, SEPs, or profit-sharing plans. This leaves only taxable accounts to invest the difference in premiums between the term and permanent policy.

Permanent life policies can have a fixed premium where a portion of the premium is allocated to a tax-deferred account called the cash value, and a portion is allocated to the cost of the policy. For many people, permanent life policies are too expensive. However, physicians often have higher incomes, placing them in a high tax bracket. So, a permanent life policy can be a very appropriate long-term product to diversify a financial plan. This is especially true if you meet the following criteria:

- You have a need for life insurance
- Your income is too high to qualify for a Roth IRA contribution, or you are phased out of the Roth IRA
- You are funding your current qualified plan at the maximum level
- You will have a significant net worth now or at retirement
- You have additional discretionary dollars that can be used for long-term financial security
- You are looking for additional ways to defer investment income from tax
- You want to be able to spend more of your other retirement assets without the fear of leaving nothing to your heirs

A sound strategy is to fund a policy right at or just under the modified endowment limits. This maximizes the accumulation portion compared to the insurance expenses.

There are many types of permanent life insurance. It is advisable to make sure the kind you are considering is designed for your intended use, whether it be family protection, estate planning, business continuation, or supplemental retirement income. As of the writing of this book, states such as Florida, Texas, Kansas, Illinois, New York, and Massachusetts also protect 100 percent of the policies' cash value or equity in the event of a judgment against you. Other states provide partial protection. Depending on your level of concern, this issue should also be considered when determining how to structure your life insurance.

This is one of the most complex financial products in the marketplace, so be sure you work with a competent, knowledgeable, and experienced advisor.

Life insurance products contain fees, such as mortality and expense charges, and may contain restrictions, such as surrender periods. Policy loans and withdrawals may create an adverse tax result in the event of a lapse or policy surrender, and will reduce both the cash value and death benefit.

Please keep in mind that the primary reason to purchase a life insurance product is the death benefit.

Disability Insurance

When you break down a financial plan and the desire to become financially independent, your income and savings level will determine your success. If your ability to earn an income is interrupted, the plan will fall apart quickly unless you protect yourself.

The odds of a long-term disability (lasting ninety days or longer) are six to seven times greater than a death during your working years. Financially, a long-term disability is worse than death, because your expenses rise and you are still around. Early in your career, the only way to guarantee your income will not stop if something happens to your ability to earn an income is to insure yourself with a quality occupation-specific disability insurance policy. By occupation-specific, this means if you cannot perform the duties of your specialty, you will be compensated. Other important features to make sure you include in your policy are the following:

- **Future Purchase Option:** This option allows you to add coverage to your policy in the future without medical underwriting. With disability insurance being quite difficult to obtain due to stringent underwriting, this is particularly important. The following are some examples of issues that can make it difficult to obtain or increase a personal policy:
    - History of mental/nervous/stress counseling
    - Diabetes
    - Excessive speeding tickets/DWI
    - Back pain, chiropractic concerns
    - Elevated liver enzymes
    - Abnormal weight

- **Guaranteed Renewal/Non-Cancelable Policy:** Once the policy has been issued, the company cannot change your rate or cancel the policy. It is a unilateral contract, meaning only you can make a change to the policy.

- **Inflation Protection:** This option makes sure that if you file a claim, the monthly benefit will increase with inflation. Over twenty-five years, at only 3 percent inflation, a $200,000 income will need to grow to $418,000 to have the same purchasing power, and that increase needs to be protected.

- **HIV Positive Protection:** If your specialty puts you at a higher risk for HIV, you will want to make sure your policy recognizes HIV as a disability. Many do not.

- **Residual Disability Benefit:** This option ensures that if your injury or illness limits your ability to practice only partially, the policy will pay a partial or proportionate benefit. Without this option, the policy only pays if you are totally disabled from your occupation.

- **Catastrophic Disability Benefit:** This option pays an additional benefit if you meet the company's definition of a catastrophic disability. A catastrophic disability is a disability that will not only cause you to be unable to work in your occupation, but would most likely require additional care either at home or in an assisted living or nursing facility. If a disability is this severe, it could result in a significant increase in your living costs at a time when your income is lower than it was while you were working. The catastrophic rider helps offset the cost of the increased level of care. This option normally adds $10 to $20 per month to the cost of your policy.

Disability insurance is not an exciting area of planning, but until you have accumulated enough money to retire, it is one of the most important fundamental financial considerations. A disability policy will keep your financial life in order in the event of a disability, but should not significantly impact your ability to save for the future.

We are now seeing a trend where medical schools are providing group policies to protect their students in the event of disability. These policies provide a reduced amount of coverage for the first- and second-year students and a larger benefit for the third- and fourth-year students. Some of these policies also offer up to $150,000 of student loan repayment in the event of permanent disability.

It is also typical for many large group practices to provide disability coverage for you. These policies typically will cover about 60 percent of your income. If the practice pays the premium for you and deducts the cost as a business expense, the benefit paid by the insurance company to you in the event of a claim will be considered taxable income.

If the group policy is not portable, or you would like more of your income protected than 60 percent, you should obtain an individual policy.

Remember, you get what you pay for. Searching the Internet for the cheapest insurance policy often results in coverage that will not protect you and your family adequately. A competent insurance agent or financial planner can provide a valuable service and should be used. They can be the best resource in helping you maximize your coverage at appropriate prices. At claim time, they can help you with the paperwork. Choosing someone you trust, especially someone who comes recommended from a reliable source, will prove invaluable.

Umbrella Liability Coverage

As your assets grow, it is wise to expand your umbrella liability insurance coverage. The limits built into most homeowner and auto policies are minimal. This coverage actually protects you and your assets in the event you or a family member cause harm due to your negligence. You are also protected in the event of negligence on your property. During residency, you should maintain at least $1 million in umbrella coverage. Once in practice, $2 to $5 million is recommended. The cost is normally around $100 to 150 per million of coverage per year. In addition, be sure to ask your agent for excess umbrella liability coverage for uninsured/underinsured motorists. This coverage protects you and your family for negligent acts caused by others.

You should also review you overall financial plan to see what assets are at risk in the event of a lawsuit. Unfortunately, we live in a society where successful or wealthy people are targeted for lawsuits more than other groups. As a physician and business owner, you are also subject to risk. In the next chapter, we will discuss asset protection planning in greater detail.

Business Continuation Planning

The focus of this section is to discuss the basics of structuring a business continuation plan for your private practice. This is a very detailed topic, and we will address the main issues. We are assuming everyone has made arrangements for their business liability, property, and equipment, and we will focus on the less understood risk management issues. With any small business, the untimely passing, disability, retirement, or termination of an owner or partner can present significant financial challenges.

When you buy in or become a partner, you will normally adopt and sign a shareholder agreement. In the agreement, the partners will typically specify what will happen in the event of a death, disability, or termination of one of the partners. Normally, the partners will mutually agree to buy out the deceased, disabled, or departing partner's interest for a specified value based on a formula. It is important to update your valuation periodically.

Without a well-designed strategy, there can be conflicts between the remaining owners and departed owners or heirs relating to distribution of income and the sale of the business. It may also be difficult for the remaining owner(s) to quickly come up with the funds to buy out the departed owner's interest. A well-designed business continuation plan will provide funding for the deceased, disabled, terminated, or retired partner's shares in the practice. This can be done through the use of life insurance, savings, or disability buyout coverage.

In the event of death or disability in a professional corporation, it is very important to have this structured properly due to the limitations that limit stock ownership to licensed practitioners only. The best way to guarantee that money will be available is to have life insurance and disability buyout insurance in place on all the partners sufficient to cover the buyout.

In the event of death, the most common types of arrangements are the stock redemption and cross-purchase strategies. The following briefly summarizes each option.

Stock Redemption

- The corporation is the owner and beneficiary of the life insurance.
- The cost of the policies is spread among the shareholders.
- If you are using permanent life policies, the cash values are subject to corporate creditors.
- Only one policy per shareholder is required (which is advantageous for large groups).
- The death benefit may be subject to the alternative minimum tax.
- Subject to COLI disclosures.

Cross-Purchase

- Shareholders own and are the beneficiaries of the life insurance policies on their partners.
- The cost of insurance is higher for younger shareholders who pay for policies on the older partners.
- Cash values are subject to the shareholders' creditors in most states if you are using permanent policies.
- The death benefit is not subject to the alternative minimum tax.
- Increased cost given multiple policies.

For larger groups, it is common to use the stock redemption strategy, and in practices with three or fewer owners, a cross-purchase plan can work well.

Business Overhead Expense Coverage

If you are unable to work for an extended period of time, the results on your practice can be devastating. You should review your situation to see if your practice could withstand the loss of revenue you or your partners generate. If the loss of the revenue would result in financial difficulty, it is advisable to purchase a business overhead expense policy. These policies pay the overhead of your practice if you or a partner is disabled. Most policies begin to pay in thirty, sixty, or ninety days, and pay for twelve to twenty-four months. The goal is to keep your practice viable financially, so you can resume working when you recover from your disability.

According to the Health Insurance Association of America, 30 percent of all people age thirty-five to sixty-five will suffer a disability for at least ninety days, and about one in seven can expect to become disabled for five years or more. The average duration of a disability lasting more than ninety days, beginning prior to age sixty-five, is four years, and four months for ages forty to forty-four, four years and seven months for ages forty-five to forty-nine, and four years and six months for ages fifty to fifty-four.

Make sure the policy will pay if you cannot perform the material duties of your specialty. A policy that pays if you cannot do any occupation is not acceptable for a physician.

Expenses normally considered as business expenses would include the following:

- Compensation and employer-paid benefits
- Salary of a non-family member hired to replace you
- Rent and lease payments
- Utility costs
- Maintenance and service
- Legal and accounting fees
- Property and liability insurance
- Malpractice and business insurance
- Professional dues
- Business debt and interest
- Business property taxes
- Supplies
- Postage

If you are starting a practice or expect your practice to grow, you should add a future increase option to your policy. This option allows you to add more coverage to your policy without having to answer any medical questions. The increase is subject to financial review only.

Disability overhead expense policies are deductible as a business expense. Most policies have a waiting period of thirty, sixty, or ninety days, with the shorter waiting period being more expensive. The policy should be for the amount of overhead you are responsible for. Some insurance companies will limit the amount of coverage you can apply for to $25,000 per month.

You should also select a benefit period that matches your situation. The benefit period sets the number of months the policy will pay. The most common benefit periods are twelve, eighteen, or twenty-four months. You can also add additional options to the policy, such as the residual disability rider. This option assures that the policy will pay if you are partially disabled but still able to perform limited duties.

Disability Buyout Insurance

A disability buyout policy will provide a lump sum to your business partner(s) or the practice in the event of a long-term disability to you or your partner(s). This will ensure that the disabled partner receives a timely buyout, and it provides the necessary liquidity to the practice to buy out the disabled partner. Many practices insure the buyout at death of a partner, but do not consider the impact of a partner that is disabled and can no longer practice or generate revenue. Financially, the impact is just as significant. Statistically, a thirty-five- to fifty-five-year-old male is almost twice as likely to become disabled than die, and a female age thirty-five to fifty-five is nearly three times as likely to become disabled.

As the group grows in size, the odds of a disability among partners increases. The size of the assets to buffer the shock to the group should also grow. See the chart below showing the probability of at least one long-term disability prior to age sixty-five.

	Number of Owners				
Age	2 lives	3 lives	4 lives	5 lives	6 lives
25	36.5%	49.4%	59.7%	67.8%	74.4%
35	34.2%	46.7%	56.7%	64.9%	71.5%
45	31.1%	42.8%	52.5%	60.6%	67.3%
55	23.4%	33.0%	41.4%	48.7%	55.1%

As the group grows to ten or more, the odds are over 90 percent that one partner will be disabled for ninety days or longer. (Source: 1985 Society of Actuaries DSP Experience Tables)

Buyout policies have a waiting period that requires the disability to last a specified period of time before paying the lump sum. The most common waiting periods are one year, eighteen months, or two years. The waiting period also prevents a buyout from occurring too soon. It should be fairly clear after eighteen months if the disabled partner is recovering, and whether the buyout should happen.

If you or your partner(s) work until a normal retirement age, you should also address other issues, such as:

- How will the practice buy out the retiring partners?
- What will the retiring partner do in regard to life and health insurance?
- How will the tail malpractice coverage be handled?

A well-designed business continuation plan will help facilitate and fund the sale of your practice in the event of a premature death or disability, and in the event of a long, healthy life.

In many cases, insurance is thought of as a "necessary evil." You have to have it, but it only benefits you if you have a claim. We look at insurance coverage as a valuable part of an overall comprehensive financial plan. The peace of mind you have by knowing you and your family are covered is worth a lot. In addition, you can be more aggressive with your other savings and investments, because you know your risk management needs are taken care of.

Malpractice Coverage

Malpractice insurance should be reviewed periodically whether you are an employee of a large group or practicing in a private practice. At a minimum, make sure you have at least the average amount of coverage recommended for your particular specialty. It is also helpful to know whether you have an occurrence or claims made policy. An occurrence policy covers you if your policy was paid up at the time the incident at issue occurred. A claims made policy covers you only if you have a policy in place when the incident occurred and when you are sued.

Looking back to the Middle Ages, we get a glimpse of the importance of insurance. People of wealth built fabulous castles and filled them with treasures. They always devoted significant resources to protecting those assets in the form of an army, a moat, and so on. In a sense, that was an early form of an insurance policy. So, as you continue to build your net worth, you should review and update your insurance to be sure you are maximizing your coverage and protecting you and your family, and your wealth.

7

The Capital Accumulation Stage

This stage represents a large amount of assets you will build up over your lifetime. The assets that tend to comprise this stage are quite varied. Some of the investments include individual stocks and bonds, mutual funds, variable life insurance cash values, and equity in real estate or your practice. Aside from the equity you build into your retirement plan, the majority of your financial independence will come from these investments. While these assets can also serve as emergency reserves, the investment horizon is usually five years or longer.

Keep in mind that all investments have risk. However, there are varying degrees and types of risk. The risk most often associated with an investment involves a fluctuating principal or a sudden depreciation in the stock market, as in October 1987 or the bear market of either 2001–2002 or 2008–2009. A corporate bond or government security holds the risk of loss of principal due to an increase in interest rates. Even a safer investment in a money market fund has some fluctuation risk and purchasing power risk, because after taxes and inflation are figured in, your dollars could be worth less than when you originally invested. A summary of the types of risk is found towards the end of Chapter 3.

Saving money is one of the most important criteria in assuring financial success. As your income increases, get in the habit of allocating at least 20 percent of your gross income to debt reduction and/or investments. By living below your total income, your net worth will potentially grow substantially, and you will cultivate a responsible attitude toward your money. Keeping up with the Joneses has become a national epidemic, but the real truth is that the millionaires next door don't concern themselves with flaunting their wealth, which explains why they are wealthy.

Generally speaking, real estate has long been a favorite investment tool for its tax benefits and as a buffer against inflation. Although there can be significant investment benefits in the long term, buying real estate is not without its risks. Deflation may decrease property values, or suspected long-term growth in a given area may not occur. Changes in tax law may reduce or eliminate anticipated tax benefits. Also, real estate is not liquid, so the necessity of a quick sale may require a substantial reduction in price.

The terms "stock" and "share" both refer to a partial ownership interest in a corporation or equity. As a stockholder, you'll be able to vote for the company's board of directors and receive information on the firm's activities and business results. You may share in "dividends" or current profits.

Investors typically buy and hold stock for its long-term growth potential. Stocks with a history of regular dividends are often held for both income and growth. As the long-term growth of a company cannot be predicted, the short-term market value of the company's stock will fluctuate. If your financial need or your fear causes you to sell when the market is "down" (also called a "bear market"), a capital loss can result. If the market is "up" (also called a "bull market"), the investor can realize a capital gain when selling.

While stocks represent ownership in a business, bonds are debt issued by institutions such as the federal government, corporations, and state and local governments. At the bonds' "maturity," the principal amount will be returned. In the meantime, bond holders receive interest. When first issued, a bond will have a specified interest rate, or "yield." If a bond is traded on a public exchange, the market price will fluctuate, generally with changes in interest rates.

Using a mutual fund is an excellent way to lower your risk, because you are diversifying through a number of stocks. A properly designed mutual fund portfolio is generally the most appropriate method of accumulating wealth at this point in the financial pyramid. Some funds have high "market risk," meaning they can fluctuate quite dramatically. Past experience shows funds that have the most risk have upside and downside potential that needs to be carefully considered. Funds with low market risk often have "inflation risk." These funds usually produce lower returns that may not keep up with inflation.

If your investment horizon is relatively short (up to five years), a more conservatively balanced fund, equity income fund, or even a medium-term corporate bond or government securities fund, will likely be the most appropriate. When your investment horizon is longer, growth-oriented stock funds are generally going to be the best choice. Again, each circumstance is different, and the advice of a competent professional will be valuable. Most firms have a short investment attitude questionnaire you can answer to help determine the appropriate asset allocation strategy that meets your needs.

Diversify! Diversify! Diversify! Nothing else will be as crucial to your portfolio as diversifying and having a long-term vision. It's important to diversify not only by asset class, but also by tax treatment and time horizon. We all know the proverb "Don't put all your eggs in one basket." Well, take it to the extreme—don't put all the baskets on the same truck, and don't drive all the trucks down the same road. It's not necessary to look too far back to recall the faddish investing in technology and startup companies of the late 1990s. Too many investors lost too much when the overvalued stocks plunged, and those eager investors expecting big returns were left with substantial losses. This also occurred as real estate became overvalued due to speculation and cheap credit during the first six years of the 2000s. The focus then shifted quickly to commodities as commodity prices soared 200 percent or more from early 2007 to mid 2008 only to drop precipitously during the recession of 2008–2009.

Sometimes misunderstood, the main goal of diversification is not to maximize your return, but to minimize your risk and lower your volatility. The basic premise is that there is as much risk in being out of the market when it goes up as being in the market when it goes down, especially for your long-term money. As an example, take the period between 1926 and 2004, a period of 924 months. If you were out of the market during the thirty top-performing months—about 3.6 percent of the time—you would have ended up with a return similar to treasury bills. While diversification does not guarantee against loss, it is a method used to manage risk.

Some additional strategies to employ when investing include dollar cost averaging and portfolio rebalancing. Dollar cost averaging is the process of investing a fixed amount of money each month (or quarter, or year) without worrying about whether the market is up or down. When it is down, you will buy more shares, bringing your average share price down. Over time, besides the element of forced savings, you will hopefully see returns you are happy with.

Using a dollar cost averaging strategy for the long term also allows you to view market downturns as opportunist, not victim. While accumulating wealth, your goal is to acquire shares. As market prices drop, the number of shares you buy for the same dollar amount increases. For example, if you were saving $3,000 per month in July 2008 into a hypothetical diversified stock investment with a share price of $30 per share, you acquired $100 shares that month. In March 2009, that same diversified stock investment may have had a share price of $15, so your $3,000 investment would have bought 200 shares. If the market rebounds to $25 per share, your initially $100 shares are worth $2,500, but the 200 shares acquired at $15 per share are now worth $5,000 and your total investment of $6,000 is worth $7,500. During the years you are saving or buying shares, you want to buy as many shares as possible at the cheapest price, and therefore a bear market can be a great opportunity for those with patience.

*Dollar cost averaging does not assure a profit, nor does it protect against loss in declining markets. This investment strategy requires regular investments, regardless of the fluctuating price of the investment. You should consider your financial ability to continue investing through periods of low price levels.

When there is a large amount of money to invest, coming up with an investment policy and adhering to it is a must. Once an overall asset allocation mix is chosen based on your goals and objectives, stick to it and change only if there are significant changes in the economy, the portfolio, and/or your goals and objectives. Then, on a regular basis, either quarterly, semiannually, or annually, rebalance the portfolio back to the asset allocation you started with. With this strategy, your investment mix does not get skewed towards more or less risk and volatility. Many current portfolio managers have the capability of providing this rebalancing process on an automatic basis.

A well-balanced portfolio is properly diversified by the following asset decisions:

- Growth stocks: large, medium, and small[1]
- Value stocks: large, medium, and small
- International stocks: developed countries, emerging markets[2]
- Fixed income: corporate bonds, government bonds, high-yield bonds
- Real estate: real property, low correlation with stocks [3]

There are many good resources to turn to that will help you take this process much further than the scope of this book. We think some of the best information can come from a competent and qualified financial advisor who will listen to you and develop a plan that meets your needs.

In general, a higher investment risk is best for those who:

- Can accept short-term losses
- Can buy shares during a down market
- Believe gains will offset losses over the long run
- Will not leave the investment if one or two bad years occur
- Have a long investment time horizon

---

[1] Investments in smaller company and micro-cap stocks generally carry a higher level of volatility and risk over the short term.
[2] Investment risks associated with international investing, in addition to other risks, include currency fluctuations, political and economic instability, and differences in accounting standards.
[3] Investment risks associated with investing in the real estate fund/portfolio, in addition to other risks, include rental income fluctuation, depreciation, property tax value changes, and differences in real estate market values.

The best way to learn sound market advice is to listen to the experts. The following quotes from mutual fund leaders all stress the futility of market timing:

Peter Lynch: "My single most important piece of investment advice is to ignore the short-term fluctuations of the market. From one year to the next, the stock market is a coin flip. It can go up or down. The real money in stocks is made in the third, fourth, and fifth year of your investments, because you are participating in a company's earnings, which grow over time."

Warren Buffet: "I do not have, never have had, and never will have an opinion where the stock market will be a year from now."

Sir John Templeton: "Ignore fluctuations. Do not try to outguess the stock market. Buy a quality portfolio and invest for the long term."

Shelby Davis: "You make most of your money in a bear market; you just don't realize it at the time."

So, to drive it home, invest for the long term and be patient.

Variable life insurance, variable annuities, and mutual funds are sold only by prospectus. The prospectus contains important information about the product's charges and expenses, as well as the risks and other information associated with the product. You should carefully consider the risks and investment charges of a specific product before investing. You should always read the prospectus carefully before investing.

8

The Tax-Advantaged Stage

The focus of this stage is to try to significantly delay, reduce, and/or minimize the impact of taxes on your financial picture. Why? To accumulate and create the highest net worth you possibly can. One method of delaying the tax involves investing dollars into qualified retirement plans. This means the dollars are made on a before-tax (qualified) basis. Again, the taxes are not eliminated. They are just deferred until the funds are withdrawn. These plans include individual retirement accounts (IRAs), simplified employee pensions (SEPs), tax-sheltered annuities (TSAs), pension and profit-sharing plans, 401(k) plans, 403(b) plans, and so on. We will discuss qualified plans for practices later.

The main advantage behind these plans is that the government has given you a significant motivation to save money. This is because your taxable income is reduced dollar for dollar by the contribution, which will then save you 20 to 45 percent of the deposit in taxes, depending on your income. In other words, your adjusted gross income is less, which means your taxable income is reduced. If you have taken care of the *Security and Confidence Stage* of your plan, you should always contribute to the 401(k) or qualified plan up to where the employer matches those funds if you plan to be at your current job long enough to be vested. Ideally, funding your qualified plan to the maximum level is a great strategy to accumulate wealth and reduce your current taxes.

While these accounts are good places to defer and delay the tax liability during your working years, they present some problems at retirement.

Remember, you aren't eliminating the tax, you are deferring it. The general principal is to save money into these plans when you are in a higher tax bracket, and withdraw the funds at retirement when you are in a lower tax bracket. However, if you do a good job saving in these plans, you may not be in a lower tax bracket at retirement due to the large amounts of money you will be pulling out of the plan when you retire. Transferring qualified assets to heirs can also present some tax nightmares if not handled carefully. Currently, income and estate taxes, when combined at the death of the second spouse, can run higher than 75 percent on qualified plans.

This is why it is very important if you are going to accumulate significant wealth that you diversify not only your investments, but the taxation of your investments. If you have aspirations to pass on money to your children or a foundation, church, university, or any other entity, it is important to compliment qualified plans with assets that pass more efficiently. Examples of this can be a non-qualified asset like a stock or mutual fund that receives a stepped up basis at death or life insurance that will pass income tax-free. These assets will still be included for estate taxes if owned personally.

For the resident physician or fellow, qualified plans are normally not a great option unless they are matched. Assuming you will be in a higher tax bracket in retirement than in training, you would not want to deduct your contribution on the 25 percent bracket and pull it out at retirement and pay 40 percent tax. A Roth IRA would be a wiser choice at this stage, assuming you have adequate cash flow, and no high-interest rate debt.

The reason the *Tax-Advantaged Stage* belongs above the *Capital Accumulation Stage* and *Security and Confidence Stage* of the pyramid is because the money deposited into these plans is normally not available until you reach the age of fifty-nine and a half. There are methods of getting your money out early. (If you qualify for one of the exceptions provided in the IRS Code.) However, money flowing into these plans should be regarded as retirement money that cannot be touched until then. There are state consequences for early withdrawal (prior to age fifty-nine and a half and not held for five years).

Calculating Your Tax Bracket

We have taken the tax code and narrowed it down to two pages (see pages 67 and 68). This is, of course, a basic guide only, just for educational purposes, and it doesn't factor in some of the specifics such as child care, student loan interest deductions, moving expenses, and so on. But surprisingly, this is fairly accurate in estimating your federal tax liability.

It's important that you work with your accountant anytime you have a major change in your life that will affect your taxes. Family changes such as a birth, death, or marriage all affect the tax you owe. Financial changes such as a new job, a raise, going back to school, and buying or moving to a new house will also impact your tax liability, and a new calculation should be made. Compare your calculation to the amount you are having withheld from your paycheck, and if you are withholding too much, change this with your employer by filling out a new W-4 form.

This is especially useful if you are graduating in May or June and starting employment mid-year. If you don't work with your employer on the correct tax withholding, they will take out an amount that would correspond to you working for the whole year. Generally, there are many expenses, and having a higher take-home pay would most likely be more beneficial than getting a tax refund the following spring.

There are some important basic points to understand about taxes. First, getting a large refund isn't really all that smart. It means you just gave the government an interest-free loan for the year. If you are a terrible saver and use this as a forced savings plan, I'm guessing it still backfires on you because you know the lump-sum tax refund is coming and you have plans for spending that amount too. In any event, I suggest you estimate your tax liability in advance and try to end up about even. That avoids any under-withholding penalties and any unexpected tax liability due that you may not be prepared for.

The second point is that it is always in your best interest to make more money. We've heard people say, "I just got a raise (or a bonus, or whatever) and it jumped me into the next tax bracket, so I'm going to take home less!" That's not how it works. The tax system is a progressive tax, and the more income you make, the more you take home. It's just that each additional dollar is taxed at a higher percentage, but the first dollars are taxed the same. Repeated, moving into a higher tax bracket affects the last of the dollars you earn, but the first dollars are still taxed at the same rate.

As an example, let's look at the Basic Federal Tax Estimator on the next page. Plug in your income (wages, interest income, etc.) and subtract contributions to pre-tax accounts to get your adjusted gross income. From that, you subtract your personal exemptions and either the standard deduction or your itemized deductions, whichever is higher. Then look up your tax bracket on the chart. The tax bracket is the tax on each additional dollar you earn, or the tax that is saved by virtue of reducing your taxable income by a dollar.

Suppose you are married and starting in a practice and your **taxable** income (after deductions) is $225,000. Let's look at how you progress though the 2009 federal tax brackets. The total tax is calculated as follows:

	The tax is:
First $16,700 of taxable income:	$1,670 (16,700 × .1)
$16,700 to $67,900 of taxable income:	$7,680 (51,200 × .15)
$67,900 to $137,050 of taxable income:	$17,287.5 (69,150 × .25)
$137,050 to $208,850 of taxable income:	$20,104 (71,800 × .28)
Remainder of income up to $225,000:	$5,329.5 (16,150 × .33)
Total Federal Tax:	**$52,071**

Basic Federal Tax Estimator

This is a guide only and is current as of 2009. For the most current basic worksheet, see www.basictaxestimator.com. This does not factor in child care, student loan interest deductions, medical expenses, moving, and so on.

Gross Income: Wages, Interest Income, etc.   _____

Minus: **Adjustments:** IRA, 401(k), TSA, etc.   _____
                                                                      =

Equals: **Adjusted Gross Income (AGI)**   _____

Minus:

       Personal Exemptions ($3,650 × # in household)
       (Phased out as income exceeds certain limits)   _____

And the higher of:
       Standard Deduction
       (Single: $5,700; Married: $11,400)   _____

Or

       Itemized Deductions

             ☐   State Income and/or Local Taxes

             ☐   Home Mortgage Interest and
                    Property Tax

             ☐   Charitable Contributions

Equals: **Taxable Income**   =
                                                                      _____

Federal Income Tax Due: (See tax table below.)

2009 Individual Income Tax Rates

Single				Married Filing Jointly			
$ -	to	8,350	10%	$ -	to	16,700	10.00%
8,351	to	33,950	15%	16,701	to	67,900	15.00%
33,951	to	82,250	25%	67,901	to	137,050	25.00%
82,251	to	171,550	28%	137,051	to	208,850	28.00%
171,551	to	372,950	33%	208,851	to	372,950	33.00%
372,951	+		35%	372,951	+		35.00%

As you can see, the higher your income, the larger percentage you pay in taxes. The higher your tax bracket, the more beneficial qualified plans or pre-tax plans offered through your employer can be. We will also look at pre-tax plans you can set up if you are self employed. If you are looking for additional ways to reduce your taxable income, some big tax deductions can come from qualified plans set up through your practice. A qualified plan will be appropriate if you want to reduce taxes, save for retirement, and/or reward and retain good employees. Qualified plan assets are also protected from creditors.

Some possible drawbacks of qualified plans as referenced earlier are:

- The money is generally not available without penalty until age fifty-nine and a half (although there are exceptions to this rule).
- All distributions are taxed as ordinary income when received.
- Setup and annual administration fees can be high.
- Upon death, the combined taxes can be over 75 percent for large balances when you add in the current income tax and estate taxes if the proceeds are paid to a non-spouse, non-charity beneficiary.

Here is a brief discussion of the various retirement plans.

Simple IRAs

A Simple IRA is often the starting point for a physician who may be moonlighting in residency, contracting themselves to a hospital, or owning a small private practice. The setup fees and annual maintenance fees are minimal. A Simple IRA allows for any owner or employee to contribute up to $11,500 in 2009, pre-tax, as long as $11,500 does not exceed 100 percent of income. The employer must also choose a matching contribution of 1 to 3 percent per year or a flat 2 percent contribution for any eligible employees. For example, if the practice chose a 3 percent match and a employee making $30,000 contributes 3 percent of his or her income to the plan, the practice would need to contribute 3 percent as well, or $900. The practice would also make a matching contribution to the owner(s). The match is immediately vested. Vesting refers to a schedule that can be placed on certain retirement plans that requires employees to work for a specified period of time before the money contributed to the plan by the employer is theirs if they leave.

401(k) Plans

A 401(k) plan is similar to a Simple IRA plan, with the main differences being contribution limits, vesting schedules (subject to non-discrimination testing), and fees. In 2009, you can defer up to $16,500 into a 401(k). If you had a 401(k) with a 3 percent match, assuming $160,000 income, the total funding could be $21,300 ($16,500 + [$160,000 × 3 percent] = $21,300). You can also have a vesting schedule on the matching contribution. This means matched contributions would not be available to employees if they left the practice within a certain time period. A normal vesting schedule is 20 percent in the first year grading to 100 percent in five years. 401(k) plans do require more monitoring than Simple IRAs. It is important to make sure your employees are contributing to a basic 401(k) plan, or your plan may be deemed top-heavy, which limits your contribution amount.

Safe Harbor 401(k) Plans

A Safe Harbor 401(k) cannot be deemed top-heavy. It functions like a traditional 401(k), except the practice is required to make a contribution of 3 percent of compensation for everyone eligible. This is not a match. It is a required contribution and is vested immediately. If the employer is willing to contribute 3 percent of eligible payroll, the top-heavy testing is not necessary, and the highly compensated owner can contribute the maximum amount each year.

Profit-Sharing Plans

Profit-sharing plans are qualified plans where employers can make discretionary contributions that may vary from year to year. Each employee receives the same contribution percentage, unless the plan is designed to take advantage of permitted disparity rules. Some of these permitted changes to contribution amounts for participants can be based on age or integrated with Social Security.

It is also possible to assign classes to employees. These permitted disparity rules allow owners to allocate a higher percentage of the dollars to the older or more highly compensated people in the practice. This will typically be the owners and associates. The contributions are usually based on business profits, but according to the IRS rules, you can also contribute to your plan based on compensation.

The maximum deductible contribution that can be made to a profit-sharing plan is 25 percent of eligible compensation, to a maximum of $49,000 in 2009. Eligible compensation is all the compensation an employer pays to eligible plan participants during the employer's tax year. Contributions are tax-deductible, and earnings accumulate on a tax-deferred basis. The employer takes the deduction for this contribution. The employer's contribution to each employee's account is not considered taxable income to the employees for the contribution year.

In very profitable practices or specialty clinics, it is common to see a profit-sharing plan together with a Safe Harbor 401(k). Together, the limit is still $49,000. This way, the owners can contribute the $16,500 throughout the year plus the 3 percent safe harbor contribution and determine at the end of year if they want to contribute the remaining balance to max out the plan at $49,000.

Simplified Employee Pensions (SEP IRAs)

An SEP IRA is very similar to a basic profit-sharing plan, and it is a good choice for a moonlighting physician and/or locum tenants, or if you are contracting your services to a hospital or health care facility. The contribution limits are essentially the same. However, you are not allowed to put a vesting schedule on an SEP IRA. Once a contribution is made for an employee, the employer may not recoup any of the contribution if the employee terminates employment. You must include all employees who have worked in three of the last five years. You are permitted to allow more immediate access to the plan, but not more restrictive access. SEPs can be a good choice if you are the only employee and your staff is limited.

If you are self-employed or a partner in a practice and have not reviewed your qualified plan in the last three years, it would be advisable to look at your options. There have been many changes to qualified plans with recent legislation, making these plans much more attractive. It is important to have a clear vision of what you want the plan to accomplish before reviewing things. An owner would consider these two main questions:

- Do you want the plan to maximize your contribution with the lowest required contribution for your staff?
  Or
- Do you want to fund the plan so it is a retirement plan for you and your employees? In this case, you fund their accounts heavily in addition to yours, and the plan provides a significant benefit to the owner and the employees.

For those who have an interest and your cash flow allows setting aside more than $49,000 per year pre-tax, there are additional options such as cash balance plans. These plans normally make sense only for very productive practices with owners over the age of forty-five, and a small number of young employees. If you are getting a late start in your planning, we would strongly suggest you look into these plans.

Roth IRAs

Assuming you have all of your *Security and Confidence Stage* issues taken care of, and your income is such that you can use Roth IRAs, we would recommend it. The Roth IRA is a very attractive option during your training if you have the cash flow to fund it. You have the ability to pay taxes on your contribution at your lower residency or fellowship income tax bracket, pay no tax as the account grows (hopefully, it grows), and you can pull the entire balance out tax-free when you are potentially in a much higher tax bracket at retirement. Would you rather pay tax on the seeds going into the ground or the end-of-the-year harvest? The seeds, of course!

Generally, growth in a Roth IRA may not be withdrawn tax-free until reaching age fifty-nine and a half and maintaining your Roth IRA for a period of five years. Keep in mind that withdrawals of your investment growth not meeting this requirement are subject to a 10 percent early withdrawal penalty. Roth IRA limits are $5,000. To fully contribute to a Roth IRA, your adjusted gross income needs to be less than $105,000 if you are single and $166,000 if you are married. You are able to do a reduced contribution up to $120,000 of adjusted gross income if single and $176,000 if married. In most cases, a young practicing physician will have an income that is too high to allow for a Roth IRA. But if you have the cash flow and qualify during school, or your first year out, then by all means, set up a Roth IRA. Then when your income is too high to qualify, you can achieve some similar results by funding a permanent life insurance policy, as discussed in Chapter 6.

In summary, qualified plans are an integral part of your retirement, and there are many ways you can design a plan. It is important to make sure your advisor fully understands all the plan design options to create a plan that maximizes the benefits you want and minimizes negatives.

There are also substantial tax benefits with a variety of non-qualified investments. The term "non-qualified" means there is no immediate tax deduction when contributing to these accounts, but the tax benefits can be very beneficial over your lifetime. The following assets are generally part of the *Capital Accumulation Stage*, but we'll provide the discussion of the tax reduction strategy of each technique in this chapter.

Stocks

As stocks appreciate in value (for this discussion, we'll assume they appreciate), there is no tax due on the appreciation until the stock is sold.

Along the way, if any qualified dividends are paid, the tax rate is less (15 percent for the highest tax bracket) than if it was the ordinary income tax rate. In addition, when the stock is sold, if held for over a year, the gain is taxed at the lower 15 percent capital gain rate. So, there is a benefit of tax deferral during the holding period and tax minimizing due to the gain being treated as a capital gain.

Real Estate

Real estate can be an excellent method of building wealth. Getting away from rent and into your first home is one obvious way. Another is leveraging the equity you have in your existing real estate into additional property. The growth is tax-deferred, and there are some favorable strategies available upon the sale and/or disposition. As for financing your house, contrary to popular belief, it can sometimes make sense to put little money down and stretch the mortgage out (and the tax deduction) in favor of freeing up cash flow for other goals and objectives.

Life Insurance

Cash value accumulation on some life insurance policies can offer retirement benefits in addition to the death benefit. As an accumulation tool, there is a cost for the insurance, so this is appropriate for someone who is younger and in good health and has a longer investment time horizon. The cash values grow tax-deferred and can be accessed tax-free, if structured properly. It is generally best to avoid having the policy become a modified endowment policy, and working with a very knowledgeable insurance or financial professional is a must.

Life insurance products contain fees, such as mortality and expense charges, and may contain restrictions, such as surrender periods. Policy loans and withdrawals may create an adverse tax result in the event of a lapse or policy surrender, and will reduce both the cash value and death benefit.

Having a permanent life insurance policy can help you maximize your overall net worth in some other ways too. You reduce your need for term insurance. In fact, the most beneficial time to have a permanent life insurance policy in place is at retirement because of all the advantages it provides. Briefly, you can be more aggressive in using and enjoying your other assets, because the life insurance essentially provides a permission slip to do so. You are also building an asset that can be passed on very efficiently to the next generation, and will provide immediate cash to pay taxes on your other assets. This is particularly important if your plan has large illiquid assets such as real estate that may need to be sold by your heirs to cover the tax if not planned for properly. Work with your financial advisor to coordinate this with your overall financial plan.

State-Sponsored 529 College Plans

There are a number of methods of putting investments in your children's or grandchildren's names. If the funds are ultimately to help them with their future college education expenses, a 529 Plan may be the answer. Some states allow a state tax deduction on the contributions, and all of the plans grow tax-deferred. If the funds are withdrawn for tuition, room and board, and "qualifying" education needs, the funds can be withdrawn tax-free also. These funds can even be transferred between family members. For a lengthier discussion, as well as a link to your state-sponsored plan, go to www.savingforcollege.com. However, make sure your own financial security is assured and your financial pyramid is sound before aggressively putting money into your children's accounts.

Your state of residence may offer state tax advantages to residents who participate in the in-state plan. You may miss out on certain state tax advantages, should you choose another state's 529 Plan. Any state-based benefits should be one of many appropriately weighted factors to be considered in making an investment decision. You should consult your financial, tax, or other advisor to learn more about how state-based benefits (including any limitations) would apply to your specific circumstances. You may also wish to contact your home state's 529 Plan program administrator to learn more about the benefits that might be available to you by investing in the in-state plan.

A 529 Plan is a tax-advantaged investment program designed to help pay for qualified education costs. Participation in a 529 Plan does not guarantee that the contributions and investment returns will be adequate to cover higher education expenses. Contributors to the plan assume all investment risk, including the potential for loss of principal and any penalties for non-educational withdrawals.

Annuities

An annuity is marketed by an insurance company as their answer to other investments. There are numerous benefits of non-qualified annuities as another financial instrument. Namely, they grow tax-deferred, and for variable annuities, you can switch between the separate accounts in a variable annuity without current income tax implications, and there are some death benefit guarantees to protect the value for your heirs. Withdrawals from annuities prior to age fifty-nine and a half are subject to a 10 percent early withdrawal penalty, as well as potential deferred sales charges. You also will want to review the asset protection laws of your state to see if annuities are protected. They are in numerous states, thus increasing their attractiveness as an investment.

Variable life insurance, variable annuities, and mutual funds are sold only by prospectus. The prospectus contains important information about the product's charges and expenses, as well as the risks and other information associated with the product. You should carefully consider the risks and investment charges of a specific product before investing. You should always read the prospectus carefully before investing.

An annuity is a long-term, tax-deferred investment vehicle designed for retirement. If the annuity will fund an IRA or other tax-qualified plan, the tax deferral feature offers no additional value. They are not FDIC/NCUA insured, bank guaranteed, or insured by any federal government agency. Variable annuities have additional expenses such as mortality and expense risk, administrative charges, investment management fees, and rider fees. Variable annuities are subject to market fluctuation, investment risk, and loss of principal. The guarantees of a variable annuity are based on the claims-paying ability of the issuing life insurance company. The guarantees and the claims-paying ability do not have any bearing on the performance of the investment options within a variable annuity.

What Do You Do at Retirement?

Estimating your retirement needs is an important factor to consider at this stage of the pyramid. A financial planning rule of thumb is to assume you will live on 70 to 80 percent of your pre-retirement income, although more and more people are enjoying a retirement lifestyle that matches their working years. This figure should be based on the income you plan to be earning at retirement, not that which you're making today. To estimate this, look at your current expenses and subtract the expenses and savings that will not be needed at retirement, and add in extra expenses (travel, medical, etc.) that may be needed then. Consider the following:

- Will you still be paying a mortgage?
- Will you still have children in college?
- Do you anticipate hefty medical expenses for yourself or your spouse?
- Do you wish to travel extensively?
- Will your day-to-day living expenses be similar, or less, than what they are now?

It is important to understand how your life will change at retirement, and establish a retirement plan that will allow you to enjoy retirement and provide you with flexibility to deal with the changes.

9

The Speculation Stage

The Speculation Stage involves risking money you can afford to lose. Some people are never comfortable with this, and thus should not consider it. These people should simply build their financial pyramid wider. This stage can involve different things for different people. It may mean investing into a small business you're starting, or investing in a friend's business. It could be buying very speculative individual stocks or aggressive specialty mutual funds.

Subjecting your money where the principal has a high degree of volatility and risk has potentially high returns, but your money could also be lost completely. It is appropriate that this stage fits at the top of the pyramid, because if the money is lost, it won't be devastating to your overall financial plan.

A good rule of thumb when deciding how much to risk in a business opportunity or other aggressive venture is one year's worth of net worth growth. Never invest more than that! In a worst case scenario, if you lost the entire amount of your investment, you have basically lost one year's worth of financial progress. While not fun, it is not financially devastating. People get into trouble and can't recover financially when they take a lifetime's worth of savings and gamble with it.

As an example, let's say your net worth is $200,000, and conservatively projected a year from now, it will be $225,000. This growth could be from additional savings, reducing debts, and/or growth from your existing assets.

In any event, the $25,000 projected growth is the maximum amount that should be considered for a very speculative investment.

In the event that an opportunity has come along which requires more than this amount, do not be tempted to risk more. Consider lowering your investment, delaying the timing until your net worth has grown, or involving a financial partner. The following ideas are just a few examples of possibilities that exist:

- Buying individual stocks of new companies
- Buying stock in initial public offerings
- Buying stock on margin (Be very careful!)
- Investing in a friend's or family member's new business
- Buying raw land and/or real estate for speculation
- Trading commodities (Be careful here!)

In summary, no one has ever gotten into trouble financially by being too conservative for too long. Sure, there are some potential lost opportunity costs, but you can get into a lot of financial trouble by being too aggressive with too much money. That's why the financial pyramid is such a useful tool to help organize and prioritize these decisions.

10

Estate Planning with Asset Protection Strategies

Asset protection planning should not be viewed as a strategy to avoid paying legitimate and reasonable creditors, but as a process to protect your personal assets from unreasonable creditors. "Unreasonable creditors" are those who bring frivolous lawsuits or get unreasonable jury awards related to medical malpractice or personal liability claims such as automobile or slip-and-fall accidents. These unreasonable creditors do exist. They are the predators looking to sue anyone who is successful. It could be any legal action where a valid claim simply doesn't exist.

In general, "asset protection" is about putting up barriers in front of the unreasonable creditors to make it difficult or impossible for them to get your personal and business assets. The key questions are:

1. What should I do?
2. When should I do it?
3. How far do I need to go?

What Should I Do?

The first step in navigating through the asset protection choices is to get educated. This chapter is not intended to be an exhaustive treatise on asset protection, but a primer to get you going in the right direction. It also is not intended to be legal advice and should not be taken as such. It is for information purposes only. Before implementing any asset protection strategy, you should consult with an attorney licensed to practice law in your state.

Exempt Assets

The first line of defense against unreasonable creditors is the protection you get from the state you live in. Each state, through its statutes, exempts certain assets from creditors. These assets can include all or a portion of the following:

- *Home:* In many states, you get an exemption from creditors for your home. This, however, is usually not an unlimited exemption, and in some states (New Jersey, for example) there is no exemption at all. Other states (such as Florida) give an unlimited exemption, meaning a creditor cannot force you to sell your home to pay off a judgment no matter what the value is. While these two states present both ends of the spectrum, the bulk of the states fall somewhere in between. An example is Minnesota, where the statute allows you to protect $200,000 of equity in your home. If the difference between your home's market value and all mortgages is greater than $200,000, a creditor can force you to sell your home, paying to the creditor any amount over the exemption.

- *Life insurance:* Some states will protect life insurance partially or entirely. This can be both the cash value and/or death benefit.

  o States such as Texas protect all of the cash value paid into a life insurance contract. This means a creditor cannot force you to withdraw funds to pay off a debt.
  o To contrast the laws of Texas, Minnesota only protects death benefits of $20,000 if paid to the surviving spouse or child and cash value of $4,000. Any amount above these can be reached by a creditor. Check with your local attorney in the event that this has changed.

- *Annuities:* Annuities are similar to life insurance. Each state decides how much, if any, can be protected from creditors.

- *IRAs:* IRAs are also given a certain amount of protection by state laws, and the protection varies from state to state. Again, it can be all, nothing, or somewhere in between. The trend, however, is for greater protection to be given to these types of accounts. You should stay tuned as these laws are changing, as you can see by Congress recently passing new bankruptcy legislation that included provisions for increased protection of Traditional and Roth IRAs owned by a person in a bankruptcy proceeding.

- *ERISA-governed retirement plans:* These plans are most commonly employer-sponsored profit-sharing/401(k) plans. They are different from IRAs in that they are governed by federal law instead of state law. In most cases, federal law will trump state laws, including judgments that require an ERISA-governed plan to liquidate assets to pay a creditor.

An attorney licensed in your state should be contacted to determine what protections your state will give you against the unreasonable creditor.

Basic Estate Planning: Wills or Revocable Trusts

The foundation for any asset protection strategy is to have your basic estate plan in place. The two primary documents you can choose from for your basic estate plan are the will or the revocable living trust. While neither of these estate planning documents give much asset protection during your life, they can (if properly drafted) give good protection to your heirs.

The Will

Having a will does not avoid probate. It is an instruction manual to the probate court on how your probate-eligible property should be distributed, who should do it, and, if your children are under the age of majority, who should be their guardian. While you are alive, it does nothing to give you asset protection as you continue to own your property in your name. It may give some asset protection to your heirs, depending on the complexity of the planning.

The probate process is designed to be a creditor's forum. Any known creditors must be given notice, and there is a waiting period for creditors to stake their claim.

The Revocable Living Trust

A revocable living trust is an alternative to using a will for your primary estate planning documents. Having a properly funded revocable living trust will avoid probate. While it will avoid the probate process, it offers limited protection of your assets from creditors. It can, however, if correctly drafted, give good asset protection for your heirs after your death.

The fact that the revocable living trust, if properly funded, avoids the probate process and the creditor-friendly rules that come with it, is reason enough to choose them over wills for your basic estate planning vehicles.

Family Limited Liability Companies and Family Limited Partnerships

One of the more common strategies used in asset protection to build upon the basic estate planning is the (family) limited liability company (FLLC) or (family) limited partnership (FLP).

FLLC

An LLC is a new form of business entity that has become increasingly popular. It combines the liability protection of a corporation with the tax and asset protection advantages of a general partnership. All fifty states have enacted LLC laws, with most of them looking and feeling like a general partnership. Some states (Minnesota, in particular) have taken on the feel of the corporation with the two levels of management (governor and manager). This feature makes it ideal for the family LLC, because it allows husband and wife to maintain various levels of control over the company, depending on their life circumstances.

An LLC can elect to be taxed like a corporation **or** a partnership. However, the majority of LLCs today elect to be taxed like a partnership. That means these LLCs do not pay income tax. The income flows through directly to the members and is reported on their personal tax returns.

To begin the LLC, articles of organization are filed with the state in which you intend to set up the company. Some states (such as Minnesota) allow you to keep the names of the members, governors, and managers private, with only the name of the organizer being filed (in most cases, the attorney who sets up the company). Having this anonymity can provide for benefits and is an important component of an asset protection strategy.

FLP

General Partnerships

A general partnership is formed when two or more people agree to carry on a business together to make a profit. It is as simple as that, and no writing has to be made and no documents need to be filed with the state except for registering the name to be used. It is good practice, however, for any partnership to have a written partnership agreement so all partners understand their rights and responsibilities. The problem with a general partnership is that all partners are jointly and separately liable for all debts of the partnership. The general partnership should be avoided at all costs because of this liability trap. If a partnership is to be used in an asset protection setting, it should be formed as a limited partnership.

Limited Partnerships

A limited partnership consists of one or more general partners and one or more limited partners. A general partner handles the control and management of the partnership. The tradeoff for this is that he or she has unlimited personal liability for all debts and obligations of the partnership. The limited partners cannot be involved in the control or management of the partnership, but they do enjoy protection from the debts of the partnership because their liability is limited to their investments in the entity. If a limited partner does participate in the control or management of the partnership, they may lose their limited liability.

Certain business formalities must be followed to help ensure limited liability protection.

Choosing Between the Two

For many years, the FLP was the entity of choice for asset protection and the minimization of estate taxes, but since its advent, the LLC is fast becoming the entity of choice because it is more flexible than the FLP and because there is no unlimited liability for the general partners as there is with an FLP. In an FLLC, the husband and wife can be involved in the management of the company without losing their liability shield while there are no creditors. If a lawsuit arises, the spouse/defendant resigns from their management role but retains their personal liability protection (limited liability assets used in entity).

Creditors Cannot Reach Assets of an FLP or FLLC

In most states, the only remedy for a judgment creditor of an LLC or FLP is a "charging order." A charging order is a legal remedy that gives the creditor the right to receive any distributions from an FLP or FLLC. It does not give the creditor the right to become an owner or to have a say in the management of the company. The creditor only receives the distributions intended to go to the owner/debtor. If this happens, the FLP/FLLC will simply choose not to make any distributions. The poison pill, however, is that even if the FLP or FLLC does not make a distribution, the creditor is responsible for the tax consequences as if a distribution had been made when the entity is taxed as a partnership.

The idea behind charging order protection is simple enough. Owners should not be involuntarily forced into a partnership with somebody they do not choose. To get complete protection from this strategy, however, great care must be put into the operating agreement to give the maximum protection possible from creditors. Using this entity to hold the assets you most want to protect allows you to protect them from creditors.

Trusts

Irrevocable Trusts

In planning, it is important to keep the revocable living trust concept talked about separate from the irrevocable trust. The revocable living trust can be amended or revoked (you retain complete control as long as you are alive and competent), but it gives limited asset protection. On the other hand, the irrevocable trust will protect your assets (assuming the transfer of property was not a fraudulent conveyance), but you lose all control and benefit. In a properly executed asset protection strategy, they do play an important role.

One of the more common uses is to own life insurance. If the trust is created properly and all of the administrative formalities are followed, it will keep the proceeds out of a deceased person's estate for tax purposes and keep them away from creditors.

Asset Protection Trusts

A strategy that is gaining popularity is the asset protection trust (APT). An APT is a self-settled trust, meaning it is funded by the creator of the trust, who is also the beneficiary. This is different from the irrevocable trust discussed above, because in a traditional irrevocable trust, the intended beneficiary is usually the spouse or children and not the person who creates the trust.

There are two main types of APTs: the domestic APT and the offshore (foreign) APT.

Domestic APT

In many states, the self-settled APT is not allowed. But in a minority of states, recent legislation is beginning to allow such asset protection vehicles.

Eight states (Alaska, Delaware, Rhode Island, Missouri, Utah, Oklahoma, South Dakota, and Nevada) now allow some form of a self-settled trust to be set up that is outside the reach of creditors. These are very new and have yet to be challenged in court. Many legal scholars believe they are unconstitutional because of the "Full Faith and Credit" clause of the U.S. Constitution, which says, "A state is to recognize the judgment from another state." This sets up a conflict of state laws issue (the self-settled APT is exempt from judgment creditors in the state it was created) and the U.S. Constitution. This means the creditor must simply register the judgment and does not have to initiate the lawsuit over again in that state.

Until the above-mentioned conflict of laws issue is settled in court, the domestic APT should probably be avoided unless you happen to live in one of the states where they are recognized. These trusts are usually expensive to set up and administer, and they are probably not a good choice for asset protection unless you are a citizen of a state that has enacted the legislation.

Offshore APT

An offshore or foreign APT is similar to the domestic APT except the trust *situs* (location) is in a foreign jurisdiction. The Cook Islands and Nevis are two popular destinations. These trusts are self-settled, but the trustee is located in one of these foreign jurisdictions, thereby putting them out of reach of the U.S. courts. A creditor would not simply be able to register a U.S. judgment in one of these jurisdictions. They would have to initiate a new lawsuit.

While the trustee and trust may be outside the reach of the U.S. courts, the creator of the trust is not outside that reach unless he or she leaves the country. Many state and federal judges despise this setup and will do whatever is in their power to unwind this type of trust, including putting the creator of the trust in jail for contempt of court. There is a long line of cases that deal with this issue, many not favorable to the debtor. These trusts are also very expensive to set up and administer, and should probably only be used in extreme cases and not with all assets. Consult with an expert asset protection attorney before considering these trusts.

When Should I Do It?

Time should be used as an ally. Having a plan in place and implemented for a period of time before an event (judgment or death) occurs will give the plan a better chance of withstanding an attack by a creditor or the Internal Revenue Service. If you wait until a lawsuit is initiated or even after an event occurs that may cause a lawsuit to be initiated, it may be too late because any transfer may be deemed a "fraudulent conveyance" and will likely quash any asset protection strategies you implement, on the theory that their only purpose was to deny creditors their claims.

How Far Do I Need to Go?

You need to take the steps necessary to give you and your family a sense of security. Assess your risk with the cost of implementing an asset protection plan, and take the action that gives you the protection you're comfortable with. With that in mind, here are some planning rules of thumb.

Planning Rules of Thumb

The following rules of thumb are a guide to assist the physician in deciding what they should do for asset protection. However, the final decisions must weigh the risk of a lawsuit with the cost of the protection. In many cases, the tools referenced in this chapter make good sense for the physician, no matter the stage of his or her career.

1. *In medical school without children:* You may not need to undertake any estate planning at this time, but you should consult with an attorney in your area to make the final decision.
2. *In medical school with children:* If you have children, you need to take some action to get the bare minimum for estate planning. You should be considering guardians for custody of your children and trustees to handle their finances if both parents die. If asset protection concerns or will concern you, you should begin with revocable trusts. Another option is to use testamentary trusts inside of your will. Keep in mind that these techniques alone do not provide asset protection for you, though they can provide

protection to your heirs. These options are more expensive than basic wills, but it will be money well spent, as these will be the foundation of your overall plan.

3. *Residency:* If you are ending your residency, you most likely will have a low net worth and high debt load. Even though your net worth is relatively low, you should consider enlisting an attorney to help you set up revocable trusts with pour-over wills as your main estate planning tools.

4. *In practice:* If you are in practice and asset protection concerns you, you should look to implementing the following procedures if your state-given exemptions do not give you the protection you want and need:

    a. If you have substantial after-tax investments, including cash value life insurance, annuities, rental real estate, or recreational property, you should consider an FLLC.

    b. If you have an FLLC, use it for your cash value life insurance. Then you could use a separate irrevocable life insurance trust for your term insurance with total death benefits greater than $1.5 million to avoid estate taxes and protect the death benefits for your heirs.

Conclusion

If the intended goal of asset protection is to be completely judgment-proof, successful asset protection becomes extremely difficult. However, if the goal is to protect a portion of your estate against the unreasonable creditor, that goal can be obtained with the help of an experienced financial planner and attorney. Without successful asset protection planning, you will lose all assets that are not exempt if you get a judgment awarded against you. With the right planning, you will be able to build walls between you and your creditors that will improve your bargaining position and help you protect what you have worked so hard to earn.

Remember, you need to take action before there are any potential lawsuits against you. Otherwise, any actions taken may be unraveled by the courts.

As with every aspect of a financial plan, the estate planning and asset protection components are extensive and need to be coordinated by a professional advisor. The advisor should obviously be very knowledgeable, but also one who listens to you and your goals, and then communicates your options…so you can work together.

You've worked hard to educate yourself in your field. We hope that this book provides you with a framework to begin your financial plan, and that you achieve all of your goals and dreams.

Disclaimers and Other Documents

The U.S. Treasury Department requires us to advise you that to the extent that this message or any attachment concerns tax matters it is not intended or written by our firm to be used, and cannot be used by any taxpayer, for the purpose of avoiding any penalties that may be imposed under the Internal Revenue Code or any other law.

It should be stressed that asset protection is a complicated area of law. Consequently, you should discuss your specific situation with a qualified asset protection attorney.

What Is IRS Circular 230?

The Treasury Department and the Internal Revenue Service have been engaged in an effort to curb abusive tax shelters. As part of this effort, they have issued final regulations under IRS Circular 230 "…to restore, promote, and maintain the public's confidence in those individuals and firms…" who act as tax advisors. It's important to note that we are not tax or legal advisors. You should seek the advice of your own tax and legal advisors regarding any tax and legal issues applicable to your specific circumstance.

This is an explanation of how our correspondence with you (including e-mails) will be affected by new IRS regulations governing tax practitioners. The new rules in effect require us to add certain standard language to many of our letters, memos, e-mails, and other correspondence concerning federal tax matters. You have probably already seen similar language on written communications from your other correspondence. Although the specific wording may vary depending on the circumstances, you can expect to see notices similar to the following:

IRS Circular 230 Notice:

To the extent that this message or any attachment concerns tax matters it is not intended or written by our firm to be used, and cannot be used by any taxpayer, for the purpose of avoiding any penalties that may be imposed under the Internal Revenue Code or any other law.

The new rules require such notices to be "prominently disclosed," i.e., "readily apparent" to the reader. The notice must be in a separate section (but not in a footnote) of the correspondence. Also, "fine-print" notices won't work. The typeface used must be at least the same size as the typeface used in any discussion of facts or law.

A practitioner who fails to satisfy the requirement of the new rules risks censure, disbarment, and substantial penalties.

Please be assured that this new policy does not reflect any decrease in the quality of our services or the amount of thought we put into our correspondence with you.

11

Contracts, Agreements, and Other Considerations

In this chapter, we will discuss some key points to understanding and clarifying associate contracts, and summarize some advantages and disadvantages for different types of practices. We strongly encourage all physicians to utilize an attorney who is familiar with medical employment contracts. You want to eliminate any surprises. A common way to create misunderstanding is to wait until you are concluding your training to start looking for a practice and then rush through the contract negotiation phase. To avoid this, we recommend that you begin looking for a practice at least six to twelve months prior to finishing. Here are some important contract points to understand:

Initial Terms

The initial terms will define when you start working and the length of employment. Many initial contracts will be for one year. If you have an interest in buying into the practice or becoming a partner, make sure all of the details are laid out. Also, determine a date for the valuation of the practice to be established and how the valuation will be determined. A valuation will normally use a three-year production average in addition to market conditions and other factors. If these terms are not discussed and put in the initial contract, the buy-in can be delayed, or worse yet, the whole practice can be broken apart.

Initial Salary Guarantee

A guarantee is normally stated as a base monthly or annual income. This can vary widely, depending on your specialty. You will likely have a production component to your income as well. This is based on your productivity, and is over and above your base salary. The production is normally paid as a bonus monthly, quarterly, semiannually, or annually. The sooner this is paid, the sooner you can get it working for you. Learn and understand the production formula so you know how everything affects the bottom line.

Non-Compete Clauses or Restrictive Covenants

A non-compete clause or restrictive covenant is normal. It is designed to protect the hospital or practice you are joining from you leaving and creating a competitor in the area. They generally do not permit you to set up a new practice within a certain radius of the current practice for a specified length of time. The distance varies based on population density. If you are in a large city, the distance might be four to six miles. If you are practicing in a rural area, the distance could be over twenty-five miles. Be sure you understand all the details. If you work at a practice with multiple locations, occasionally the restrictive covenant will pertain to all their locations. Clarify this and make sure you know where all the locations are.

In response to many restrictive covenants not being upheld that state a time and distance limitation, we are starting to see a clause in the restrictive covenant called "liquidated damages." This is a financial penalty charged to you if you leave, and it can be in excess of $100,000. It is generally stated in terms of financial damages incurred by the practice you were at when you leave if you establish or join a practice within the stated time and distance. These are enforceable because they do not impede your right to work.

Malpractice Insurance

Malpractice coverage will normally be paid by the practice. It is recommended that associates carry the same policy their employer carries. If you are self-employed or contracting your services to a hospital or clinic, you will need to provide your own coverage. In this case, inquire as to what insurance company insures the majority of the physicians with that group.

You should also clarify who will pay for your tail malpractice coverage if you leave your practice. Tail malpractice coverage protects you and the practice from malpractice claims arising after you terminate employment.

Signing Bonus

The amount and size of signing bonuses can vary widely. However, it is important to pay attention to when the bonus is paid. If you sign with your practice in the calendar year prior to your starting date, make sure you get your bonus in the year prior to starting practice. By getting the bonus in the prior calendar year, you will owe less in taxes on the bonus, since your income will be lower.

Many bonuses are also distributed as a forgivable loan. These are not taxed when you receive them, because it is initially established as a loan. When you satisfy your contract, typically after one or two years of service, the loan is forgiven and the taxes are due in that year at your tax bracket then. It is not uncommon to have a $10,000 tax bill due on a $25,000 loan received in a prior year that was forgiven in the current year. It is important to understand if your signing bonus is a loan or taxable payment, and to plan accordingly.

Other Benefits

If you are in a group practice with many owners, it is common to have some group life, health, and disability insurance, as well as a 401(k) plan. If you are working at a small private practice, you would most likely cover those expenses on your own. It is also helpful if the private practice has a qualified retirement plan available for you. Clarifying vacation time and continuing medical education are also important to discuss to avoid misunderstanding.

The Pros and Cons of Large Group Practices versus Private Practice

Working with hundreds of physicians, we receive significant feedback from our clients as to what they like and dislike about their situation. If you have an entrepreneurial spirit and like the challenge of running a business, the private practice route may be the best situation. For those who would rather not have to deal with these things and want a little more security and stability, a group practice will be attractive. Deciding which fits you best and then going that route will make you the most satisfied professionally. Here is a brief summary of the issues, based on our experience.

Some of the benefits of a large group practice are as follows:

- There are solid group benefits, including life insurance, disability insurance, health insurance, malpractice insurance, as well as a qualified retirement plan.
- There is a consistent salary. Normally large groups offer a base salary that can be increased with production.
- Your responsibility is to provide medical services. You are not required to handle staffing issues, payroll, hiring and firing, and so on. When your work is done, you can go home.
- Your personal risk is lower, since you are not responsible for paying for the expenses of the practice.
- You share emergency calls with others in your group.

Some of the drawbacks to large group practices include:

- In the long run, your income can be lower than owning a private practice.
- You have less control over your hours.
- You may have less control over patient care, especially if the practice accepts payments from a number of insurance providers.
- You have no asset to sell when you want to leave if you do not buy in.

We see some of the following advantages in private practice:

- You have a higher potential income.
- You have complete control over how you practice.
- You have flexibility in what hours and days you will see patients.
- You are building an asset to sell at retirement.

Some of the drawbacks of private practice include:

- You have higher personal risk. You are now responsible for paying for the practice, building, salaries, supplies, and so on.
- You are responsible for the hiring, firing, and staffing issues, or you can pay someone to do it.
- You may have to provide your own insurance plans (life, disability, health, and malpractice).
- You may need to provide your own retirement plan.
- You must coordinate emergency call coverage when you are out of town.

The military also offers some competitive options. Typically, the government will pay for a large portion of your school costs. In return, you must practice in a branch of the armed services for a specified number of years when you complete school or residency. While the pay is lower than a private or group practice, your student loans are less, your medical care is covered, and you receive a housing allowance. If you have flexibility in where you live for a few years after graduation, this can be a great option.

Moonlighting

In many ways, moonlighting at an offsite facility can be very similar to operating a private practice. If the hospital or clinic you contract your services to gives you a 1099, you are considered self-employed. If they give you a W-2, you are an employee. Working as an employee requires no additional work on your end. Your taxes will be withheld and your FICA taxes will be paid.

If you get a 1099, this gives you an opportunity to deduct reasonable business expenses and reduce your taxable income. Reasonable business expenses can be business travel, continuing medical education, dues, publications, professional fees, automobile expenses, cell phones, laptops, medical equipment, food, or entertainment. If you do receive a 1099, it is wise to consult your accountant or a financial advisor familiar with moonlighting income.

It is very important to understand that if no taxes are being withheld from your checks, you should set aside at least 45 percent of your moonlighting check for taxes. This money should be kept in a separate money market or savings account. As an independent contractor, your income taxes will be higher than as an employee. This is because you must pay both sides of the FICA tax, which equals 15.3 percent, compared to 7.65 percent as an employee. This, added to the 30 percent you could already be paying, can push your effective tax rate on moonlighting income to 45 percent or higher. This is why it is important to keep track of your expenses and be organized.

It is also possible to set up a specific retirement plan for 1099 income. The most common examples would be an SEP IRA or Simple IRA, as discussed in Chapter 8. These allow you to put the income aside before federal and state taxes are paid. Most physicians moonlight to make money to spend, but if you are concerned about taxes or retirement, setting up an SEP IRA or Simple IRA could make sense.

Deciding whether to incorporate is also something you may want to consider. If you are concerned about being sued or are in a high-risk specialty, setting up a professional association, S corporation, or LLC may make sense. This will limit your liability. However, most independent contractors will be covered by the malpractice insurance of the practice they are moonlighting at. In addition, most young physicians have relatively few assets and are not an attractive target for a lawsuit.

As a physician, you have so many choices as to how you can practice. The key is finding the method that is fulfilling and rewarding to you, both professionally and personally. This gives you the opportunity to serve your community in many ways.

12

Case Studies

Observations and Overview

In this chapter, we provide five specific case studies that demonstrate the concepts outlined in this book. These will show that the pyramid of financial needs can be used in most circumstances as a method of organizing and prioritizing financial decisions. Of course, much of this is subjective, and ultimately the correct answer merges the quantitative and qualitative aspects of the decision into a financial plan you are comfortable with. We hope you find the following case studies to be a very helpful addition to the understanding of the techniques presented earlier in this book.

The following case studies are fictitious, and any similarities to any actual person(s) or situation(s) are coincidental.

Case Study #1: A Starting Point

Circumstances: Michael is in his second year of internal medicine residency and is planning another three-year cardiology fellowship. His wife Alison is a registered nurse. They have no children.

Their financials goals and concerns are as follows:

- Pay off debt.
- Accumulate savings.
- Buy a starter home.
- Start a family.
- Begin retirement savings.
- Protect themselves against loss.

The Numbers

Michael's income is $44,000 per year. Alison earns $54,000. They have $175,000 in student loans currently deferred at 3 percent interest. They have $5,000 in credit card debt and $3,000 in savings and few other assets and debts. Their take-home pay is $5,400 per month, and they currently have about $700 per month in discretionary income. Their current rent payment is $1,200.

Their Net Worth Statement

Fixed Assets:
Savings Account:	$3,000
Checking Account:	$1,000
Total Fixed Assets:	$4,000

Variable Assets:
Roth IRA:	$2,500
403(b) Balance:	$4,300
Total Variable Assets:	$6,800

Personal and Other Assets:
Vehicles:	$12,000
Personal Property:	$10,000
Total:	$22,000

Total Assets: $32,800

Liabilities:
Vehicle Loan (8%):	$6,000
Credit Cards (13.9%):	$5,000
Student Loans (3%):	$175,000
Total Liabilities:	$186,000

Net Worth (Assets minus Liabilities): ($153,200)

The Financial Plan

Security and Confidence Stage:

- Apply the majority of the surplus dollars towards eliminating the credit card debt.
- Keep federal student loans in economic hardship deferment during residency. Apply for true deferment once fellowship starts.
- Obtain a private disability insurance policy for Michael with the maximum future purchase option.
- Obtain inexpensive convertible term life insurance for both Michael and Alison.
- Have a will drafted including health care directives.
- Increase emergency reserve fund once the credit cards are paid off.
- Purchase a $1 million umbrella liability policy if/when a home is purchased.

Capital Accumulation Stage:

- Survey the real estate market for affordability and determine if a four-year timeframe is reasonable to purchase a home.
- Determine the equivalent mortgage payment to current rent payment. Due to the deductibility of mortgage interest and property taxes, it can be a large difference. In their case, the equivalent mortgage payment is $1,500, which would buy roughly a $200,000 home including taxes if financed at 6.5 percent and amortized over thirty years.
- Purchase a home for around $200,000 if suitable housing can be found in that price range.

Tax-Advantaged Stage:

- Begin Roth IRA contributions once the credit cards are paid off and an emergency reserve has been established.

- Continue Alison's 3 percent 403(b) contribution to take full advantage of the 3 percent employer match.

Summary

The plan addresses current as well as future issues. The emphasis is placed on the *Security and Confidence Stage* by eliminating the credit cards, building an emergency fund, locking in life and disability insurance, and addressing their housing situation. Since the cost is relatively small, the future income has been protected with the addition of the properly structured disability policy that allows Michael to add coverage when he enters private practice. The term life insurance policy guarantees life insurance coverage will be in place when Michael and Alison start a family. The umbrella liability policy is their first asset protection component to better protect their personal assets from liability. The Roth IRA and 403(b) serve as building blocks to their investing and retirement needs.

Case Study #2: The Thirty-Five-Year-Old Physician Couple

Circumstances: Jennifer finished her residency five years ago and has been working hard to pay off debt and get established in her practice, while balancing time with her family. Her husband Robert, a pharmacist by training, has been home full-time with their two children, ages four and one. The plan is for him to go back to work part-time when the youngest is in school.

They have many financial goals at this time, including:

- Build "the house of their dreams" in a few years.
- Continue to pay off their debts.
- Start to save for their children's education.
- Save for retirement.
- Reduce tax liability.
- Protect wealth.
- Have a plan for emergencies and unexpected events.

The Numbers

Jennifer works at a large teaching hospital as a radiation oncologist with an annual income of $350,000. She has access to the standard employee benefit package that includes health insurance, disability insurance of 60 percent of income capped at $10,000 per month, life insurance of one times salary, the ability to contribute to a tax-sheltered annuity, and so on. Their monthly take-home pay is $20,000, and their monthly expenses are $12,000, leaving $8,000 per month in excess funds with which to plan.

Their Net Worth Statement

Fixed Assets:

Savings Account:	$15,000
Checking Account:	$3,000
Certificate of Deposit:	$2,000
Total Fixed Assets:	$20,000

Variable Assets:

IRA:	$13,000
Roth IRA:	$9,000
Mutual Funds:	$10,000
Individual Stocks:	$2,000
Variable Life Cash Value:	$4,000
401(k) Balance:	$40,000
Total Variable Assets:	$78,000

Personal and Other Assets:

Home:	$375,000
Vehicle:	$20,000
Personal Property:	$30,000
Total:	$425,000

Total Assets:	$523,000

Liabilities:

Mortgage (30 years, 6%):	$290,000
Home Equity Line (7%):	$15,000
Vehicle Loan (9%):	$10,000
Credit Cards (18%):	$2,000
Student Loans (3.5%):	$110,000
Total Liabilities:	$427,000

Net Worth (Assets minus Liabilities):	$96,000

The Financial Plan

Security and Confidence Stage:

- Increase umbrella liability insurance to $3 million.
- Secure a personal disability policy on Jennifer to supplement the group coverage.
- Increase the home equity line of credit to be used for emergencies, including paying off the car so the interest is less and tax deductible. (Pay $2,000 per month toward this, and save the extra when paid off, to be used for the new house.)
- Secure life insurance using a combination of variable adjustable life policies and term life insurance.
- Pay off the credit cards immediately, and continue to stretch out the mortgage and student loans for the length of the loan.
- Draft wills, trusts, and appropriate estate planning documents.

Capital Accumulation Stage:

- Commit to saving $6,000 into the following:
- Initiate 529 Plans for children's college fund.
- Initiate a fee-based brokerage account to start building a portfolio of non-qualified mutual funds.
- Fund variable life policies up to the limits allowed, being careful to avoid having the policy becoming modified endowment contracts.
- Consider building their dream house sooner than later, to take advantage of today's lower interest rates, low down payment needed, and appreciation of higher-value property, and to allow enjoyment of the house with the family for more years.

Tax-Advantaged Stage:

- Continue to maximize the contribution into the 403(b) retirement plan ($16,500 per year), making sure this is actively managed using a carefully constructed portfolio.

Speculation Stage:

- Wait until the base of the pyramid is more established.

Summary

Their new plan takes care of "building a moat" around the financial castle they are starting to build. They feel more confident now that they have wills and appropriate levels of insurance. The life insurance plays an important role in the *Security and Confidence Stage* as well as the *Capital Accumulation Stage*, and was an excellent addition to the overall financial plan. With the risk management in order, they can aggressively begin a monthly savings plan for college and mid- to long-term financial security. In addition, they are starting to work with an architect to build their dream home, and can pursue that sooner than they imagined. They finally feel like the "lean" years of medical school and residency are starting to pay off.

Case Study # 3: On to Residency

Circumstances: Joe and Jennifer finished medical school a few weeks ago. Both matched at the same teaching hospital, Joe in urology and Jennifer in anesthesia, and are preparing for their move.

Their financial goals and concerns are as follows:

- Create a workable budget.
- Pay off debt.
- Purchase a home.
- Buy a new vehicle.
- Start a family in two years.
- Begin retirement savings.
- Protect themselves against loss.

The Numbers

Their starting salaries are $45,000 per year. They have $325,000 in student loans at 6.89 percent with their first payments due in six months. They have $10,000 in credit card debt and $3,000 in savings. Their take-home pay will be $5,900 per month, and after expenses are paid, they should have $1,550 per month of surplus cash flow available.

Their Net Worth Statement

Fixed Assets:
        Savings Account: $3,000
        Checking Account: $1,000
        Total Fixed Assets: <u>$4,000</u>

Variable Assets:
        Total Variable Assets: <u>$0</u>

Personal and Other Assets:
        Vehicle: $5,000
        Personal Property: $2,000
        Total: <u>$7,000</u>

Total Assets: <u>$11,000</u>

Liabilities:
        Credit Card (11.99%): $10,000
        Student Loans (6.89%): $325,000
        Total Liabilities: <u>$335,000</u>

Net Worth (Assets minus Liabilities):   <u>($324,000)</u>

The Financial Plan

Security and Confidence Stage:

- Apply majority of surplus monthly cash flow toward eliminating credit card debt.
- Apply amount already budgeted for student loan payments toward credit card debt to eliminate credit card debt quicker. Since the student loan balance is high and the payment schedule may be influenced by future legislation or regulations, it would be prudent to reduce other consumer debt as much as possible, to free up cash flow for other needs.
- Research purchase of new affordable vehicle that meets current needs, including the addition to the family in the next two years, and investigate financing options available.
- Obtain individual disability policies for both Joe and Jennifer with maximum future purchase option.
- Obtain inexpensive convertible term life insurance for both Joe and Jennifer.
- Once credit card debt is eliminated, shift portion of cash flow surplus to increase emergency fund to three to six months of fixed expenses.
- Purchase a $1 million liability umbrella policy once home is purchased.

Capital Accumulation Stage:

- Investigate real estate market in new location to determine if suitable home can be purchased that will accommodate needs through the full five-year duration of Joe's residency.
- Evaluate equivalent mortgage payment in comparison to rent payment in the same market. Deductibility of mortgage interest and property taxes can result in income tax savings that may make buying a home more attractive than renting. Careful evaluation of expenses and income tax consequences should be part of the

decision-making process in determining whether to buy or rent. Purchase a home for no more than two or three times annual income.

Tax-Advantaged Stage:

- Begin Roth IRA contributions once credit card debt is eliminated, emergency fund is well established, and monthly student loan payment is determined.
- Contribute at least the minimum amount needed to receive the full employer match to the 403(b) plan (or other employer-sponsored qualified plan).

Speculation Stage:

- Wait until the base of the pyramid is more established

Summary

At this stage of their careers, this plan focuses on the importance of the *Security and Confidence Stage*, laying a solid foundation or base to the pyramid. Emphasis is placed on eliminating credit card debt, increasing emergency funds, and managing student loan debt. At the same time, the couple is starting to build a solid foundation for the future by obtaining individual life and disability insurance to protect the family's income, taking care of their housing and transportation needs, and beginning a long-term savings program. With minimal cost, Joe and Jennifer have protected current and future income through the purchase of an occupation-specific disability policy with a future purchase option rider that allows them both to add significant coverage in practice without providing evidence of insurability. The term life insurance provides immediate protection to cover mortgage and guarantees coverage when they start a family. The liability umbrella is a foundational asset protection component. The Roth IRA and 403(b) are fundamental to their retirement needs.

Case Study # 4: The Final Training Year

Circumstances: Eric is in the final year of his orthopedic surgery residency and preparing for fellowship in a different state. He is single but expects to be married in one or two years, with children to follow soon after. Eric owns a home he purchased at the beginning of his residency, which he is selling. He plans to rent during fellowship. Other than his mortgage, Eric has no other debt. His parents paid for his undergraduate and medical school. Eric has contributed the maximum annual contribution to his Roth IRA since he started residency, and he maintains a high balance in his checking account.

Eric's financial goals and concerns are as follows:

- Invest the profit from the sale of home.
- Start a family in two years.
- Protect himself against loss.

The Numbers

Eric's current salary is $49,000 per year. However, in two months his salary will be $52,000. His take-home pay in two months will be $3,200 per month, and after expenses are paid, he should have $1,000 per month of surplus cash flow available.

His Net Worth Statement

Fixed Assets:

     Checking Account: $11,000

     Total Fixed Assets: $11,000

Variable Assets:

     Roth IRA: $22,000

     403(b): $6,500

     Total Variable Assets: $28,500

Personal and Other Assets:

     Home: $142,000

     Vehicle: $5,000

     Personal Property: $2,000

     Total: $149,000

Total Assets: $188,500

Liabilities:

     Mortgage (6.25%): $129,000

     Total Liabilities: $129,000

Net Worth (Assets minus Liabilities): $59,500

The Financial Plan

Security and Confidence Stage:

- Maintain emergency fund such as savings account, interest-bearing checking account, or money market for funds currently held in non-interest-bearing checking account. The balance of the cash flow surplus, after acquiring the necessary insurance programs noted below, should be committed to the same account for future expenses such as additional down payment on next home, wedding, and so on.
- Obtain individual disability policy with maximum future purchase option.
- Obtain inexpensive convertible term life insurance.
- Purchase a $1 million liability umbrella policy.

Capital Accumulation Stage:

- Upon the sale of home, deposit proceeds in a secure interest-bearing account, such as a savings account, certificate of deposit, or money market. Funds will then be readily available to use for down payment on home purchase in fourteen months.

Tax-Advantaged Stage:

- Continue maximum Roth IRA contributions in current year, and in the subsequent year if the combined income from a partial year fellowship and partial year in practice does not exceed the Internal Revenue Service income limits.
- Contribute at least the minimum amount needed to receive the full employer match to the 403(b) plan (or other employer-sponsored qualified plan).

Speculation Stage:

- Wait until the base of the pyramid is more established.

Summary

At this stage of his career, the plan focuses on the importance of the *Security and Confidence Stage*, strengthening the foundation or base of the pyramid. Emphasis is placed on building a solid foundation for the future by maintaining sufficient liquidity for future expenses and obtaining individual life and disability insurance to protect him and his future family's income. With minimal cost, Eric has protected current and future income through the purchase of an occupation-specific disability policy with a future purchase option rider that allows him to add significant coverage once he is in practice without providing evidence of insurability. The term life insurance he acquires when he is insurable will provide immediate protection for when he starts a family. The liability umbrella is a foundational asset protection component. The Roth IRA and 403(b) are fundamental to their retirement needs.

Case Study #5: Partnership on the Horizon

Circumstances: Michael finished his fellowship three years ago and has been diligently saving for his practice buy-in, retirement, and the children's education while balancing time with his family. His wife Katharine has been home full-time with their two children, ages five and four. Katharine also has a small home-based business. However, the business does not generate a substantial income. The income generated is used to fund trips to activities related to her business.

They have many financial goals at this time, including:

- Fund practice buy-in.
- Buy a mountain home in the next five years.
- Save for their children's education.
- Save for retirement.
- Reduce tax liability.
- Protect wealth.
- Have a plan for emergencies and unexpected events.

The Numbers

Michael works for a radiology practice and is about to make partner. His annual income prior to partnership is $325,000. His anticipated first-year partner income is $525,000. He has access to the standard employee benefit package that includes health insurance, disability insurance with a monthly benefit of 60 percent of income to a maximum $10,000 per month, life insurance in the amount of one times salary, and the ability to contribute to a 401(k) plan with an employer match to reach the annual maximum. His current monthly take-home pay is $19,000, and their monthly expenses are $16,500, leaving $2,500 per month of surplus cash flow. However, when partnership income begins, the cash flow surplus is expected to be $9,000 per month.

Their Net Worth Statement

Fixed Assets:

Money Market Account:	$99,000
Checking Account:	$2,000
Fixed Life Cash Value:	$2,100
Total Fixed Assets:	$103,100

Variable Assets:

IRA:	$41,750
Roth IRA:	$14,750
Mutual Funds:	$3,300
Variable Life Cash Value:	$50,200
401(k):	$29,000
Total Variable Assets:	$139,000

Personal and Other Assets:

Home:	$750,000
Vehicle:	$30,000
Personal Property:	$400,000
Total:	$1,180,000

Total Assets:	$1,422,100

Liabilities:

First Mortgage (30 years, 6%):	$570,750
Second Mortgage (30 years, 6%):	$144,000
Student Loans (5.375%):	$86,000
Total Liabilities:	$800,750

Net Worth (Assets minus Liabilities):	$621,350

The Financial Plan

Security and Confidence Stage:

- Increase umbrella liability insurance to $5 million.
- Increase personal disability policy on Michael to further supplement the group coverage.
- Increase life insurance coverage for Michael and Katharine using a combination of heavily funded and minimally funded cash value policies and term insurance.
- Continue making regular payments on the mortgage and student loans. Once partnership income begins, may evaluate whether to accelerate some of the debt, depending on the other goals and cash flow needs. For example, depending on the projected cost of the second home and prevailing interest rates, reducing second mortgage will increase total deductible mortgage amount available for the purchase of the second home.
- Borrow money for practice buy-in on balloon loan, and deduct interest expense from K-1 income.
- Review wills, trusts, and appropriate estate planning documents drafted during fellowship in a different state.

Capital Accumulation Stage:

- The balance of the cash flow surplus, after making improvements in the insurance programs noted above, should be committed to the following savings programs:
  - Initiate 529 Plans for children's college fund.
  - Initiate a fee-based brokerage account to start building a portfolio of non-qualified mutual funds.
  - Continue funding variable life policies to take advantage of tax-deferred accumulation of cash values under current laws, but keep in mind the funding limits to avoid having a policy turn into a modified endowment contract.

   o   Consider purchasing their second home sooner than later, if interest rates are favorable, a low down payment is needed, and the expenses can be worked into the budget. This enables the couple to enjoy more years in the home with their family, and depending on market conditions, may enjoy appreciation of higher property values.

Tax-Advantaged Stage:

- Continue to maximize the contribution into the 401(k) retirement plan, making sure this is actively managed using a carefully constructed portfolio.
- Maximize profit-sharing plan contribution. Coordinate the limit with the 401(k) plan. Use an actively managed account with a carefully constructed portfolio.

Speculation Stage:

- There is sufficient cash flow to consider more speculative investments once partnership income level is achieved, if this meets the client's investment objectives and risk/return tolerance.

Summary

Their new plan enhances their previous strategy and solidifies the base of their financial pyramid. They have confidence that the buy-in can be achieved, a sense of security that their ability to generate an income and protect their family are ensured through higher amounts of disability and life insurance, their assets are protected with the increased liability umbrella, and clarity in the updated wills. The life insurance plays an important role in the *Security and Confidence Stage* as well as the *Capital Accumulation Stage*, and was an excellent addition to the overall financial plan. With the risk management in order, they can more aggressively save for college, retirement, and other mid- to long-term financial goals. In addition, they are considering purchasing the mountain home sooner than five years. They feel confident that the years of medical school, residency, and fellowship are generating significant returns, and they feel secure in their financial future.

13

Conclusion

The medical profession is a wonderful career choice. It offers flexibility in how, what, when, and where you want to practice. The combination of these factors gives you so many financial choices. The decisions you make financially should be based on your own personal and business goals. What makes sense for a friend's career may not make sense for you. The type of college savings plan you set up may be different than your neighbor's. The life insurance you choose may not be the same as your business partner's if you have different life goals or cash flow. The decisions you make need to be based on what *you* value most in life.

A successful financial plan should work under all scenarios, things that occur in real life. In the event that you live a long, healthy life, you want your plan to provide income to you throughout retirement and maintain your lifestyle. If, unfortunately, things do not go as planned, your financial plan should protect you, your family, your employees, and your assets. The plan should work to accomplish your goals as effectively as possible. This means growing your net worth efficiently, enjoying life, minimizing taxes, and managing your risks. A good financial plan will not only address the financial aspects of your life, but will also provide valuable assurance that you are properly preparing for your retirement.

Having a properly designed financial plan and a relationship with a trusted financial planner will be a source of comfort and strength. The assurance in knowing you have planned for contingencies is not something that can be quantified in dollars. It is something that can only be experienced. We hope this book gives you the information you need to start putting your financial affairs in order or finish what you may have already started.

14

Additional Resources

Glossary of Financial Terms

Annuities, Fixed	A vehicle marketed by an insurance company that pays a guaranteed rate of return.
Annuity, Variable	An investment marketed by an insurance company with premiums mostly converted into separate accounts invested in stocks, bonds, and money market accounts.
Assets	An investment or property that has value.
Assets, Fixed	Those assets that do not have a major loss of principal. These would include the most conservative assets in your portfolio, like checking and savings accounts, money market funds, certificates of deposit, T-bills, EE savings bonds, whole life insurance cash values, etc.
"Bear" Market	A period of time in which securities are declining in price.

"Bull" Market	A period of time in which securities are rising in price.
Capital	Money or other assets.
Certificate of Deposit	An account at a bank, savings and loan, and/or credit union that pays a fixed rate over a certain period of time.
CFP®	Certified Financial Planner™: A person who advises others on achieving long-term financial goals, either for a fee or on a commission basis. Ethics and professional standards are monitored by the CFP® Board: www.cfp-board.org.
ChFC	Chartered Financial Consultant: A degree emphasizing investments and tax planning earned through the American College.
CLU	Chartered Life Underwriter: A degree in insurance and risk management earned though the American College.
Debt	Owing money.
Deferment	A six-month grace period granted to federal student loans at the conclusion of medical school. Economic hardship deferment can be offered after your initial deferment if you qualify financially. If you qualify, your loans can remain in deferment for up to another three

	years. During any deferment, only your unsubsidized loans accrue interest.
Diversification	Spreading your risk among various accounts to reduce volatility.
Dollar Cost Averaging	The buying of a fixed dollar amount of stock shares at regular intervals so that more shares are bought at low prices, fewer at high, resulting in an average cost that is lower than the average price.
Forbearance	A declaration of non-payment that must be granted to residents and fellows during training. During forbearance, all your loans will accrue interest.
IRA	Individual retirement account.
Liquidity	How easy it is to convert your investment into cash.
Money Market Mutual Fund	A pool of assets invested in bank CDs, T-bills, and commercial paper, and considered the best emergency reserve account due to extreme safety and liquidity.
MSFS	Master of Financial Services: An advanced degree earned by the American College.
Mutual Fund	A general term for an open-end investment company compromised of investments in basically any category.

Portfolio	A listing of securities held by an investor or organization.
Principal	The current balance owed on a debt or the value of an account.
Sales Load	An up-front fee or commission on a mutual fund purchase used to compensate the broker or financial planner.
Securities	Investments.
Stock/Share	A certificate representing ownership in a corporation that is usually sold to raise money to begin or expand a business.
Subsidized Loan	A federal loan where the interest during school and deferment is not accruing.
T-Bills	Treasury bill—a short-term federal obligation of the U.S. Treasury sold at a discount.
Unsubsidized Loan	A loan that accrues interest during school and training.

For Further Information

The following is a very brief list of some of the resources for the individual interested in personal financial planning. To list all the helpful information available today would be a book in itself, so included here are some of the most popular, and our personal favorites. The opinions and strategies expressed in the following sources should not be acted upon without first discussing them with a qualified investment, tax, and/or legal advisor.

Newspapers

The Wall Street Journal is the most widely read business newspaper. It also has daily articles about investing and money matters.

Barron's is a weekly newspaper that reviews the stock markets. The Lipper Analytical Services mutual fund performance ratings are included on a quarterly basis. There are also frequent articles on mutual fund investing.

Investor's Business Daily is an excellent newspaper with a broad range of articles on finance, business, and the economy.

The New York Times and *USA Today* both have excellent business sections.

Magazines

Medical Economics frequently publishes articles related to financial issues concerning physicians.

Money magazine's December, January, and February issues usually have articles on tax and investment planning.

Kiplinger's Personal Finance magazine's January issue focuses on financial planning (including tax planning) for the coming year. Mutual funds are reviewed in the September issue.

Smart Money offers articles on investing and financial planning.

Forbes is a biweekly investment magazine that looks at news from an investment point of view and has an annual mutual fund survey, usually published in August.

Business Week focuses on current business news and contains articles on personal business, investing, and financial planning.

Books

The New Retirementality by Mitch Anthony is a great new book that identifies the issues facing everyone as they plan their future. This is especially helpful to those who are worried about what they will do during their retirement years.

The Ultimate Gift by Jim Stovall provides a very interesting story about wealth and the transfer of wealth to the next generation. We would suggest this book for anyone who wants to instill a sense of value and work ethic into their children, employees, and others.

Money and the People You Love by Bruce Helmer is a great overview of real financial issues families face in life. It lays out in entertaining detail how to construct a financial plan to address what truly matters in life.

Web Sites

www.ama-assn.org is the official Web site for the American Medical Association.

www.bloomberg.com offers financial market reports.

www.investorama.com lists information on thousands of online financial sites.

www.irs.gov provides information on publications and forms to answer most tax questions.

www.marshallgifford.com is co-author Marshall Gifford's Web site and lists his presentations, background, philosophies, and links to other helpful sites.

www.memag.com is the Web site for *Medical Economics Magazine.*

www.morningstar.com features a comprehensive review of mutual funds and portfolio tracking.

www.quicken.com includes a wealth of personal finance information, as well as calculators and interactive financial formulas.

www.savingsbonds.gov lists everything you need to know about U.S. savings bonds.

www.savingforcollege.com discusses the multitude of state 529 college plans available, and each of their advantages.

www.sec.gov is the official site of the Securities and Exchange Commission.

www.toddbramson.com is Todd's consulting Web site and lists his presentations, e-newsletter, and many excellent links.

www.wallstreetcity.com has just about everything you need to know about stocks, including free quotes, research, and criteria-based charts matching your specifications.

ABOUT THE AUTHORS

Marshall W. Gifford, ChFC, CLU

Chartered Financial Consultant Marshall Gifford has been working as a financial advisor in Minneapolis, Minnesota, since 1993 and consults with clients who reside across the country. He has specialized in working with physicians since 1993. Since 1993, he has worked extensively with graduates of the University of Minnesota Medical School and residency programs, as well as the residency and fellowship programs at the Mayo Clinic, Northwestern University, the University of Illinois at Chicago, and Rush University. He also works with physicians at hundreds of private practices across the United States and is the immediate past president of North Star Resource Group's medical division. He prides himself on keeping current on trends in medicine.

Mr. Gifford's financial advice has been quoted multiple times in *Medical Economics* magazine, and he has appeared on Minneapolis/St. Paul news stations numerous times as a financial expert. He is a member of the Top of the Table, reserved for the top one half of one percent of financial advisors worldwide.

Mr. Gifford is an avid athlete. He enjoys cycling, running, cross-country skiing, and wakeboarding. He played basketball for Minnesota State University at Mankato, and was ninth in the country in the decathlon in 1993. He has ridden RAGBRAI, the *Des Moines Register*'s annual bike ride across Iowa, every year since 1990, and he ran the Boston Marathon in 2003.

Mr. Gifford lives in St. Paul, Minnesota, with his wife and three sons.

Todd D. Bramson, CFP®, ChFC, CLU

Certified Financial Planner™ Todd D. Bramson has been working in the field of financial planning for over twenty years, and has been recognized as one of the 150 best financial advisors for doctors nationwide by *Medical Economics* magazine. He is one of only a few financial advisors who have been listed each of the last four times *Medical Economics* has provided this survey. An exceptional teacher, as well as a motivating author and speaker, he has been quoted in numerous financial publications, and has spent several years as the financial expert on the local NBC live 5:00 p.m. news broadcast. In June of 2004, he spoke at the prestigious Million Dollar Round Table, a worldwide organization of the top one half of one percent of all financial services professionals. He writes an e-newsletter, *The Bramson Report*, and maintains a Web site at www.toddbramson.com.

Mr. Bramson's belief, "If the trust is there, the miles don't matter," has earned him devoted clients not only in his hometown of Madison, Wisconsin, but in almost every state in the country. Along with all the advanced degrees expected of a trusted financial professional, he is committed to keeping abreast of all the developments in his field, and to playing an active role in his community. He conducts regular public seminars and is active in his church, the Evans Scholars Alumni Foundation, Blackhawk Country Club, and the Verona Area Community Theater.

Mr. Bramson is also the founder and president of Bramson and Associates LLC. Information on his company, philosophy, and services can be found at www.toddbramson.com. You will quickly see that Mr. Bramson is dedicated to providing valuable wisdom through his books, Web site, presentations, and newsletters.

William H. Montag

William H. Montag joined North Star Resource Group in 1997 upon graduation from Minnesota State University in Mankato, Minnesota. He is a partner and financial advisor in North Star's Iowa City, Iowa, office. His practice specializes in building long-term relationships with physicians based on trust, integrity, and loyalty as they transition through medical school to residency, fellowship, and then finally into practice.

Mr. Montag works jointly with business partner and fellow advisor Forrest Friedow, forming a powerful team to better serve their clients. Bill and Forrest work extensively at the University of Iowa Carver College of Medicine and the University of Iowa Hospitals and Clinics in Iowa City, Iowa, and Vanderbilt University Medical Center in Nashville, Tennessee. In addition to his work with the medical students and various residency programs, Bill has hundreds of clients in practice throughout the country.

Mr. Montag is a frequent presenter for medical students, residents, fellows, and practicing physicians at various teaching hospitals and medical practices throughout the country, focusing on the building blocks of a sound financial plan. Bill and Forrest engage their clients in a comprehensive financial planning process, centered on building financially sound habits as early as possible in their career.

Mr. Montag is a member of the Million Dollar Round Table, the Premier Association of Financial Professionals®, recognizing the top 5 to 7 percent of experts in his field. He serves as president of North Star's Medical Division, a group of advisors who work exclusively with physicians, sharing best practices and the latest trends in medicine. He is actively involved with the Iowa City Area Chamber of Commerce, where he serves as an ambassador, and he is a member of the Optimist Club and the University of Iowa I-Club.

Mr. Montag enjoys spending time with his fiancée, Lori, and his daughter, Blair, along with golfing, boating, and fishing. He is also a passionate Iowa Hawkeye fan.

Forrest M. Friedow

Forrest M. Friedow, financial advisor in Iowa City, Iowa, joined North Star Resource Group in 2000. He is member of North Star's Medical Division, a group of advisors who work exclusively with physicians, sharing best practices and the latest trends in medicine. He specializes in working with physicians beginning in their final year of medical school, through residency, fellowship, and into practice. In addition, he practices jointly with business partner and fellow advisor, Bill Montag, creating a powerful team where each can focus on his own area of specialty. Forrest concentrates on comprehensive financial planning, tailoring strategies to the unique financial circumstances of medical professionals in six primary areas: current financial position, protection planning, investment planning, retirement planning, tax planning, and estate planning.

Forrest and Bill work extensively at the University of Iowa Carver College of Medicine and University of Iowa Hospitals and Clinics in Iowa City, Iowa, and at Vanderbilt University Medical Center in Nashville, Tennessee, and they host numerous workshops for the various residency programs in each location. In addition, Forrest and Bill have hundreds of clients in practice throughout the United States and travel frequently to meet with them.

"As a guiding advocate we are able to facilitate, develop, and refine comprehensive financial strategies for our clients, positioning each individual and family for financial success!"

Mr. Friedow enjoys spending time with family, friends, and his two dogs, working out, kayaking, and is currently pursuing ordained ministry.

Robert Kaufer

Robert Kaufer has over fourteen years of experience as a practicing attorney working primarily in the areas of simple and complex estate planning, business and contract law, probate law, and residential real estate law. He received his law degree from Hamline University School of Law and an M.B.A. from the University of St. Thomas. He, his wife, and their two children reside in St. Paul. His legal philosophy is to educate the client about their options and then help them make the best choices to meet their unique goals and objectives. Mr. Kaufer is not affiliated with CRI Securities or Securian Financial Services Inc.

To contact Robert Kaufer:
Phone: 1-651-967-7932
Web site: www.kauferlaw.net
E-mail: bob@kauferlaw.net

NORTH STAR RESOURCE GROUP

Marshall W. Gifford, ChFC, CLU
North Star Resource Group
2701 University Avenue SE
Minneapolis, MN 55414
1-612-617-6119 or 1-888-257-9839
marshall.gifford@northstarfinancial.com

Todd D. Bramson, CFP®, ChFC, CLU
North Star Resource Group
2945 Triverton Pike Drive #200
Madison, WI 53711
1-608-271-9100 ext. 218
todd.bramson@northstarfinancial.com

William H. Montag
North Star Resource Group
Paul Helen Building
209 E. Washington Street, Suite 300
Iowa City, IA 52240-3928
1-319-351-4307 ext. 26
william.montag@northstarfinancial.com

Forrest M. Friedow
North Star Resource Group
Paul Helen Building
209 E. Washington Street, Suite 300
Iowa City, IA 52240-3928
1-319-351-4307 ext. 23
forrest.friedow@northstarfinancial.com

ASPATORE